Roots of Liberty

Unlocking the Federalist Papers

Edited by

Scott D. Cosenza
&
Claire M. Griffin

CONTENTS

FOREWORD

It has always been of paramount importance for America's young people to learn about the first principles that built America from a colonial backwater to the world's greatest superpower.

We intend to make a serious contribution to such knowledge with our classroom series *Roots of Liberty*, and this first volume focuses on what has been widely hailed as the greatest exposition of America's Founding principles ever written: the *Federalist Papers*.

While the U.S. Constitution has been our guiding light for over two centuries, the *rationale* behind its inception is even more significant.

The *Federalist Papers* were written by a diverse trio of Founding Fathers who were not in agreement on every issue - James Madison, Alexander Hamilton and John Jay. The *Papers* were designed as an apologia for skeptical audiences - revealing the Founders' thinking about concepts such as the proper role of the federal government, the separation of powers, and property rights. Most historians agree the *Papers* were instrumental in winning the hard-fought battle for ratification of the Constitution as the supreme law of the land.

This treasure trove of wisdom has long been inaccessible because of the exhaustive nature of its content and arcane language. We attempt in this volume to accomplish what the subtitle suggests: unlock the wisdom and power of the *Federalist Papers* for countless generations of young Americans.

The ultimate goal of our project is to strengthen America's civil society by helping our future leaders understand that the principles embedded in the U.S. Constitution are as relevant today as they were when the Constitution was ratified in 1789.

This volume has been authored by a team of constitutional experts - we call them the "dream team" of constitutionalists - and designed to both bring the past alive and explain its contemporary relevance. These collected essays are supplemented by substantial digital, audio-visual, and interactive content written for students of varied abilities.

borrowing money or raising troops. Congress could not tax citizens directly and instead had to make requests of the states for funds. Rather than entrusting power to a single executive when it was out of session, a committee consisting of one delegate from each state kept the government running while the others were home taking care of personal affairs.

The Articles, of course, were not perfect. The Confederation government lacked certain critical powers. The system of state requisitions often produced revenue shortfalls, especially after Cornwallis surrendered to General George Washington in October 1781. Without a steady stream of revenue, the Confederation had difficulty paying its debts and, because of the dismal shape of public credit, would have been unable to obtain loans if an emergency arose. Foreign powers were reluctant to deal with the Confederation Congress inasmuch as it could not ensure that states and individuals would respect treaty obligations. Congress also lacked the power to persuade foreign powers to comply with existing duties or to respect American rights.

Prelude to the Convention

These shortcomings were accentuated by several events in the mid-1780s. First, the British refused to vacate key fortifications because the states ignored treaty provisions prohibiting impediments to creditors' recovery of debts. British merchants faced state legislation that effectively nullified the debts owed and they quickly complained to Parliament. In responding to protests from the British government, Congress was unable to persuade the states to repeal the debt-relief legislation.

Second, independence did not bring the prosperity expected by the commercial states of the union. Merchants envisioned new markets opening and handsome profits to be earned. They did not foresee natural trading partners such as Britain and France imposing discriminatory restrictions on American trade. Without a power to regulate interstate or foreign commerce, Congress could not respond with its own restrictions to force a resolution.

Third, in 1784, Spain had closed the Mississippi to American commerce. Citizens in the western part of the United States depended on the river to bring their goods to market. Spain's actions threatened the livelihood of thousands and also discouraged American expansion into the wilderness.

Finally, when debt-ridden Massachusetts farmers revolted and closed courthouses throughout the state to prevent confiscation of their property, Congress was unable to raise money or forces to assist Massachusetts in restoring order. The state's government eventually quelled the rebellion, but this episode persuaded many that the union needed a more vigorous national government.

In March 1785, delegates of Maryland and Virginia met at George Washington's home at Mount Vernon, Virginia to settle a dispute over navigation of the Potomac River and conflicting commercial regulations. The dispute was not settled, and the conference raised broader questions about the regulation of trade between the American states. The Virginia legislature then invited all thirteen states to send delegates to Annapolis, Maryland to consider commercial matters.

The Annapolis Convention met in September 1786, but only five states sent delegates. Determined that reform would occur, delegates suggested that another convention be held the next year in Philadelphia, Pennsylvania. James Madison, a Virginia delegate present at Annapolis, drafted Virginia's invitation to the other states to assemble and consider "the Exigencies of the Union." Following Virginia's lead, the Confederation Congress endorsed the idea of a convention for "the purpose of revising the Articles of Confederation."

The Philadelphia Convention

A remarkable group of individuals assembled in Philadelphia in May 1787. Almost all of the fifty-five delegates were well educated men, established in their businesses and professions, and leaders in their communities. All but a few had taken an active part in the American Revolution, more than half had served in the Continental Army. A majority of the delegates to the Philadelphia Convention had served in the Congress established by the Articles of Confederation. Several had served as state governors. Others had helped write state constitutions.

George Washington, the great leader of the Continental army in the revolution, was elected president of the Convention. Other notable Founders among the delegates included Alexander Hamilton from New York, Benjamin Franklin from Pennsylvania, and James Madison from Virginia. The most prominent Founders not present in Philadelphia were Thomas Jefferson, who was then representing the United States in Paris, and John Adams, who was serving in a similar capacity in London.

Madison Frames the Debate

As the Philadelphia Convention began its work, it soon became apparent that one of its most important members would be James Madison. Madison was very experienced in practical politics and extremely well read in history and theories of government. He was very knowledgeable about the shortcomings of confederations and weak central governments.

Madison came to Philadelphia convinced the delegates needed to do much more than merely revise the Articles of Confederation. They needed to replace the Articles with a new form of national government with new powers strong enough to defend American citizens from foreign threats and the disruptive effects of the constant squabbling in and among the various states.

Madison persuaded the rest of his delegation to back what was to be called the "Virginia Plan" for a national government of greatly expanded powers, a government capable of exercising those powers not through the separate states but directly on individual citizens through a reformed Congress, and also through a newly formed executive and judiciary. Based on the individual equality of all United States citizens, the Virginia Plan called for the representation of each state in the new Congress to be based upon the population of that state, and proposed to do away with the equal representation of states in Congress that was a fundamental part of the government established by the Articles of Confederation.

Although many delegates to the Philadelphia Convention shared Madison's frustration with the Articles, they were reluctant to support the Virginia Plan. They had painful memories of the many abuses to their lives and liberty and property that had been committed by the strong centralized authority of Great Britain. Also, the delegates from the smaller states did not want a state's representation in Congress to be based on that state's population; they wanted to maintain the equality of the states found in the Articles. To back their position, the small state delegates formally introduced what was called the "New Jersey Plan," which proposed to grant each state equal representation in the new Congress.

Compromises Great and Small

The issue of a state's representation in Congress quickly became central to the debates. It threatened to derail the entire Convention until a delegate from Connecticut introduced a compromise plan. This compromise plan, later called the "Great

Compromise," combined the basic elements of Congressional representation found in both the Virginia Plan and the New Jersey Plan. Under the compromise, Congress would be made of two chambers. Representation of the states in the lower chamber, the House of Representatives, would be based on population. In the upper chamber, the Senate, each state would have equal representation. In mid-July 1787, after much debate, the Great Compromise was narrowly approved by the delegates and the thorny issue of representation was resolved.

The delegates had saved the Convention, but much work remained. They labored through the hot, humid summer, debating, compromising, and ultimately voting to agree on each basic component or process for the new national government.

The Virginia Plan called for the president to be elected by the Congress, but the delegates feared this would make the president too dependent on the Congress. Ultimately, they decided that the president would be selected by the newly created Electoral College, to be made of members from each state, equal in number to the Senators and Representatives of each state.

The delegates explicitly enumerated, or listed, the powers granted by the people to each of the three branches of the new national government. The Congress, for example, was granted the power to tax and the power to regulate interstate and foreign commerce, thereby correcting two of the most perceived flaws with the Confederation. Congress was also granted the power to declare war. Within the newly created executive branch, the president was made commander in chief of the armed forces, and given the power to be exercised with the advice and consent of the Senate, and to make treaties and appoint senior government officials. Within the newly created judicial branch, a supreme court was established, and Congress was empowered to establish lower federal courts with powers to resolve disputes between citizens and states.

Along with representation in Congress, the issue of slavery was one of the most controversial issues to face the Convention. Delegates from southern states wanted to protect slavery and the slave trade. They wanted no interference in the slave trade, and they wanted to count slaves in the populations of their states for the purpose of determining the representation in the new House of Representatives.

Other delegates from states outside the South opposed slavery and the slave trade to varying degrees, but the delegates as a whole did not want the Convention to fail as a result of a split over these two issues. The delegates compromised on both issues. Interference with the slave trade was prohibited for a period of twenty years. For the purpose of determining a state's representation in the House of Representatives, three-fifths of the slaves in that state would be counted as a part of the state's population. Unlike the Great Compromise and other permanent compromises, the negotiations on slavery only postponed the day of ultimate resolution.

In early September 1787, the Convention neared the end of its work. The system and structure of the new national government, with the basic elements we know today, had taken shape: a government of three separate branches, each with enumerated powers to conduct its activities while checking and balancing the power of the other two branches.

At this point, George Mason of Virginia proposed a list, or bill, of rights be added to the constitution to specify and protect the rights of individual citizens. Other delegates argued such an addition was unnecessary, perhaps even unwise. They argued that none of the enumerated powers granted to the new national government threatened the individual rights already guaranteed to citizens in state constitutions. They also argued that a specific list of individual rights might be misunderstood to represent the only rights that citizens possessed. The Mason proposal was defeated, but the concept of a bill of rights would return during the ratification debates. The promise, by supporters of the new constitution to amend and add a bill of rights once the constitution itself was ratified, proved to be a commitment that was crucial to gaining the approval needed to ratify and adopt the new constitution.

The Struggle for Ratification

On September 17, 1787, the Convention delegates signed the completed constitution. Then, in accordance with its own Article VII, and with the original Virginia Plan, the constitution was submitted to the states for their consideration and approval. After the Convention, supporters of the new constitution did everything they could to build support for it. Their job was not an easy one. Many persons thought too much power had been granted to the new national government. These opponents of the new constitution became known as Anti-Federalists.

Anti-Federalists were especially active in New York State. To counter them, Madison joined with Alexander Hamilton and John Jay, both of New York, to write a series of essays placed in New York newspapers to defend and explain the new constitution. These essays, as a group, came to be known as the *Federalist Papers*. Together, the essays provided a comprehensive explanation and defense of the new constitution, making the case that the newly strengthened central government would effectively protect the interests of the nation and its citizens without threatening their natural rights to life, liberty and the pursuit of happiness. The Federalists prevailed. In the year following the

Convention, all but two states, North Carolina and Rhode Island, approved the new constitution. By 1790, these two had followed and the nation's new age of "a more perfect Union" had begun.

2

A Bulwark Against Foreign Danger

The Constitution as a Defense Against Foreign Aggression

by Christopher Donesa & Jamil N. Jaffer

Federalist Papers referenced in essay: #3, 14, 15, 24

A. In 1787, the fledgling Union was far from a global superpower. Alexander Hamilton argues that America had instead *"reached almost the last stage of national humiliation* (No. 15)." British and Spanish troops either occupied or threatened key "territories or important posts," and the national government could do almost nothing to stop them. The nation's mariners could not even freely navigate the great Mississippi River. To add insult to injury, the United States had not yet repaid its foreign debts from the Revolutionary War.

B. But if America was too young to truly command its vast explored and unexplored territories, one might have hoped its success in declaring and winning its independence from the British Empire would have earned some dignity, diplomatic respect, and influence in the world. To the contrary, however, Hamilton discovered the federal government's lack of any real power or authority to speak with one voice for the several states had led to just the opposite: *"The imbecility of our government even forbids them to treat with us. Our ambassadors abroad are the mere pageants of mimic sovereignty* (No. 15)." Although the United

d become a free and independent nation, even in the eyes
political leaders, its standing in the world could only be
described as uncertain, if not downright shabby.

C. This situation, in the view of the authors of the *Federalist Papers*, was directly tied to the weak and ineffectual form of government established by the Articles of Confederation. The most meaningful powers of any national government—the ability to raise money and armies to support the national interest and defend its territories—had been left in the hands of the states. Hamilton described the situation bluntly (No. 15): *"We have neither troops, nor treasury, nor government."* And, as a result, in Hamilton's view, the nation was in no *"condition to resent or to repel [any foreign] aggression."* The federal government even lacked the basic power to require the several states to accept the treaty ending the Revolutionary War. While the federal government established by the Articles technically had the ability to pass constitutionally binding legislation with respect to the security of the nation *"in practice [these laws were] mere recommendations which the States observe or disregard[ed] at their option."*

D. All of this was more troubling in light of the significant foreign threats still facing the nation. Because fear from foreign attack is so far from the America of today—strong, confident in itself, and secure in its possessions and interests—Hamilton's concerns bear repeating:

> *Though a wide ocean separates the United States from Europe, yet there are various considerations that warn us against an excess of confidence or security. On one side of us, and stretching far into our rear, are growing settlements subject to the dominion of Britain. On the other side, and extending to meet the British settlements,*

are colonies and establishments subject to the dominion
of Spain. This situation and the vicinity of the West India
Islands, belonging to these two powers create between
them, in respect to their American possessions and in
relation to us, a common interest.... A future concert of
views between these nations ought not to be regarded as
improbable. (No. 24)

The United States was faced with the prospect of being surrounded by forces of two historical global powers, Britain and Spain, both of whom might have reason to join with the other to evict the new government in America and reestablish themselves in the expanding Western Hemisphere. Defending against these superpowers and other foreign threats would require a single military force—a seagoing navy—ready to defend the American territory effectively, with strength and resolve.

E. The purely foreign threats weren't the only ones facing the young nation. America was faced with three separate potential conflicts: Britain and Spain and their possessions on both sides of the nation, and the Native Americans within and on the boundaries of the American territories. As Hamilton noted, *"the savage tribes on our Western frontier ought to be regarded as our natural enemies, their natural allies, because they have most to fear from us, and most to hope from them* (No. 24)." The defense of the American nation against this internal threat would require a strong and effective land-based fighting force:

Previous to the Revolution, and ever since the peace,
there has been a constant necessity for keeping small
garrisons on our Western frontier. No person can doubt
that these will continue to be indispensable, if it should
only be against the ravages and depredations of the
Indians....If we should not be willing to be exposed, in a

15

naked and defenseless condition, to their insults and
encroachments, we should find it expedient to increase
our frontier garrisons in some ratio to the force by which
our Western settlements might be annoyed. (No. 24)

F. Hamilton further argued such a fighting force would also serve to protect the nation from the additional threat posed by the British and Spanish forces already located on the American continent, as well as protect the new nation's commerce with its closest (albeit hostile) trading partners:

It may be added that some of those posts will be keys to
the trade with the Indian nations. Can any man think it
would be wise to leave such posts in a situation to be at
any instant seized by one or the other of two neighboring
and formidable powers? To act this part would be to
desert all the usual maxims of prudence and policy. (No.
24)

G. Troublingly, some of the state governments had even begun conducting their own independent negotiations with foreign nations and tribes. As noted by John Jay, this had already led to serious consequences for the nation as a whole.

Not a single Indian war has yet been occasioned by
aggressions of the present federal government, feeble as it
is; but there are several instances of Indian hostilities
having been provoked by the improper conduct of
individual States, who, either unable or unwilling to
restrain or punish offenses, have given occasion to the
slaughter of many innocent inhabitants. (No. 3)

H. The Federalists feared the situation would get worse as the individual states began to interact more aggressively and actively within the territories of the European nations on their borders.

> *The neighborhood of Spanish and British territories,*
> *bordering on some States and not on others, naturally*
> *confines the causes of quarrel more immediately to the*
> *borderers. The bordering States, if any, will be those who,*
> *under the impulse of sudden irritation, and a quick sense*
> *of apparent interest or injury, will be most likely, by*
> *direct violence, to excite war with these nations; and*
> *nothing can so effectually obviate that danger as a*
> *national government.* (No. 3)

I. Foreign affairs, defense, and trade situations of the new nation had become so dysfunctional that it was one of the highest priorities for those seeking to draft a new constitution. In Hamilton's view, the then-current *"circumstances combined, admonish [the American nation] not to be too sanguine in considering ourselves as entirely out of the reach of danger* (No. 24)."* The Constitution, as written and ratified, creates a strong, single union against external threats. This union ensures the nation speaks with one voice in the areas of commerce and foreign policy, and has the necessary military might to carry out its policies. The jealousies and passions of the several states, as well as the response to perceived slights experienced by any state, would be moderated by a strong national government. A strong, single union would better ensure the national position against foreign powers by making single decisions about when and how to go to war. *"One good national government affords vastly more security against the dangers of [foreign aggression] than can be derived from any other quarter* (No. 3)."

J. To carry out this mission, the new constitution sought to provide the new government with the clear authority to declare war, raise an army and a navy, regulate commerce with foreign nations and Indian tribes, define and punish violations of agreements between nation-states, call upon the various militias of the several states to protect the nation from both internal and external threats, and generally provide for the common defense. These provisions, combined with the provision of the Constitution, authorizing the federal government to "make all Laws…necessary and proper for carrying into Execution" these authorities, served to significantly strengthen the new federal government to protect itself and its people against threats posed by external actors. The new constitution also set limits on the ability of the states to engage in unilateral [individual] foreign negotiations restricting them from entering into compacts with other nations, prohibited them from keeping troops or warships in a time of peace or engaging in war without the federal government's consent except in very specific circumstances, and limited them in the imposition of duties and taxes on imports and exports except where absolutely necessary.

K. This new constitution created a limited, but powerful federal government, which respected the rights of the states, but had the capabilities and authorities to maintain a strong union against external threat. This Constitution was seen as a *"bulwark against foreign danger, as the conservator of peace among ourselves, as the guardian of our commerce and other common interest* (No. 14)." The document crafted by the Founders ultimately led to creation of a nation-state with the capability and wherewithal to profoundly shape the course of history, a promise that modern America continues to deliver some 225 years later.

3

The Powers Delegated to the Federal Government Are Few and Defined

The Doctrine of Enumerated Powers

by Roger Pilon

Federalist Papers referenced in essay: #14, 23, 25, 32, 41, 42, 44, 45

A. The doctrine of enumerated powers stands for the idea that Congress has only those powers that are enumerated in the Constitution, which the people delegated to Congress when they ratified the Constitution or later amended it. Thus, the doctrine is of fundamental importance. It explains the *origin* of Congress's powers, their *legitimacy*, and their *limits*. By virtue of the doctrine, the Constitution of the United States establishes a government of delegated, enumerated, and thus limited powers.

B. The *Federalist Papers* contain many discussions of the doctrine of enumerated powers, but they are often difficult to understand because they make assumptions many people today don't fully understand. And they address a variety of particular issues rather than the general theory of the doctrine. Before examining those discussions, therefore, it will be useful to first outline the Constitution's basic theory of legitimacy, especially since the doctrine of enumerated powers is so central to it, and then show how the doctrine is manifest in the Constitution itself.

C. The Constitution's theory of legitimacy draws from the theory that was first set forth in the *Declaration of Independence*. In that document America's Founders made it clear they wanted to rid themselves of British rule—which they thought was illegitimate in many respects—and to establish in its place legitimate government with legitimate powers. To make their case, they drew on the natural law tradition, stretching back to antiquity, which holds there is a moral law of right and wrong that should guide us in making actual laws. It is that moral law, especially concerning natural rights, that is referenced in the famous passage that begins, "We hold these Truths to be self-evident." Thus, the Founders first set forth the moral order as defined by our natural rights and obligations—the moral rights and obligations we would have toward each other if there were no government—and only then did they set forth the conditions for legitimate government and governmental powers. And they did it that way because they understood that governments don't just happen; rather, they are created, by human action, and so we need to know how that happens legitimately—by right.

D. To do that, notice that the Declaration's self-evident truths begin by assuming we are all equal, at least in having equal rights to "life, liberty, and the pursuit of happiness." But in holding that each of us has a right to pursue happiness, nothing more is said about what will make us happy, and for good reason—that will vary from person to person. Thus, the freedom to pursue happiness is left up to each individual, provided only that each of us respects the equal rights of others to pursue whatever makes them happy. Live and let live.

E. But we may not all agree about what our rights and obligations are. And even if we did agree, not everyone will always respect the rights of others. Either intentionally or accidentally, people will violate others' rights. The Founders understood this, so after they outlined the moral order, they turned to the political and legal order and took up the question of legitimate government: "That to secure these Rights, Governments are instituted among Men, deriving their just Powers from the Consent of the Governed." Notice the limits implicit in that language. The main purpose of government is to secure our liberty by securing our rights. But if the powers needed to do that are to be "just" or legitimate, they must be derived "from the Consent of the Governed."

F. When they drafted the Constitution eleven years later, the Framers drew on that theory of legitimacy: individual liberty, secured by limited government, with its powers derived from the consent of the governed. We see the theory right from the start, in the document's Preamble: "We the People," for the purposes listed, "do ordain and establish this Constitution." In other words, all power comes from the people. We created the government. We gave it its powers by ratifying the Constitution that sets forth its structures, powers, and protections. For those powers to be truly legitimate, however, we must first have had them ourselves before delegating them to the government to be exercised on our behalf. The Framers mostly abided by that principle, the major and tragic exception being the Constitution's oblique recognition of slavery, which took the Civil War and the Civil War Amendments to correct. For the most part, however, they established a legitimate government with legitimate powers.

G. With the Constitution's theory of legitimacy now before us, we can examine how the Framers implemented it through the doctrine of enumerated (listed) powers. To state the doctrine most simply, if you want to *limit* power, as the Framers plainly did, don't give it in the first place. That strategy is evident in the very first sentence of Article I: "All legislative Powers herein granted shall be vested in a Congress." Notice first that the subject is *all* legislative powers that are herein granted—which are the only such

21

powers in a Constitution of *delegated* powers—and they rest with the Congress. Second, the powers are "granted"—or delegated by the people, from whom they have to come if they are to be legitimate. Finally, as implied by this use of the words "all" and "herein granted," *only* those powers "herein granted" were, in fact, *granted.* In sum, Congress has *no* legislative powers *except* those that were "herein granted"—powers that are limited to those that are enumerated in the document.

H. Congress's powers are enumerated throughout the Constitution, but the main legislative powers are found in Article I, Section 8. There are only eighteen such powers. Plainly, the Framers wanted to limit the federal government to certain enumerated ends, leaving most matters in the hands of the states or the people themselves. In fact, that point was made perfectly clear when the Bill of Rights was added two years after the Constitution was ratified. As the Tenth Amendment states, "The powers not delegated to the United States by the Constitution, nor prohibited by it to the States, are reserved to the States respectively, or to the people." Where the federal government has no power, the states or the people themselves have a right.

I. The doctrine of enumerated powers was crucial to the ratification debate. The *Federalist Papers* were written to convince skeptical electors and the delegates they sent to state ratifying conventions that the new constitution was necessary and, in particular, would not give the new federal government any more power than was absolutely necessary to carry out its responsibilities. The doctrine of enumerated powers—the main restraint on the new government—was most famously stated by James Madison (No. 45):

The powers delegated by the proposed Constitution to the federal government, are few and defined. Those which are

*to remain in the State governments are numerous and
indefinite. The former will be exercised principally on
external objects, as war, peace, negotiation, and foreign
commerce; with which last the power of taxation will, for
the most part, be connected. The powers reserved to the
several States will extend to all the objects which, in the
ordinary course of affairs, concern the lives, liberties, and
properties of the people, and the internal order,
improvement, and prosperity of the State.*

J. Notice those words: "few and defined." The federal
government was to have only limited responsibilities. Most power
was to be left with the state governments. They were closer to the
people who could then better control them.

K. Madison continues, *"It is to be remembered that the general
government is not to be charged with the whole power of making
and administering laws. Its jurisdiction is limited to certain
enumerated objects, which concern all the members of the
republic, but which are not to be attained by the separate
provisions of any* (No. 14)." Madison argues there are certain
things—like national defense and foreign and national
commerce—that are properly national concerns since they are
largely beyond the competence of individual states. In fact, one of
the main reasons the Framers sought to write a new constitution
was because the Articles of Confederation afforded the federal
government too little power to deal with such matters.

L. Alexander Hamilton picks up these themes (No. 23) while
focusing on the document's aims:

*The principal purposes to be answered by union are these
- the common defense of the members; the preservation of
the public peace as well against internal convulsions as*

external attacks; the regulation of commerce with other nations and between the States; the superintendence of our intercourse, political and commercial, with foreign countries.

Opponents, he continues,

ought not to have wandered into inflammatory declamations and unmeaning cavils about the extent of the powers. The POWERS are not too extensive for the OBJECTS of federal administration, or, in other words, for the management of our NATIONAL INTERESTS; nor can any satisfactory argument be framed to show that they are chargeable with such an excess.

M. Hamilton goes on to argue (No. 25) that there are two sides to the doctrine of enumerated powers. The main emphasis in the *Federalist Papers* is to show how the doctrine will limit the size and scope of the new government. The other side, however, is to ensure the federal government has enough power to do the things that a national government will need to do. Hamilton addresses that issue cleverly, in the name of ensuring the new government will remain limited:

Wise politicians will be cautious about fettering the government with restrictions that cannot be observed, because they know that every breach of the fundamental laws, though dictated by necessity, impairs that sacred reverence which ought to be maintained in the breast of rulers towards the constitution of a country, and forms a precedent for other breaches where the same plea of necessity does not exist at all, or is less urgent and palpable.

N. Note Hamilton's word of caution. The new government's powers are to be limited by enumeration, but those who would limit them even further run the risk of sowing the seeds—necessary breaches that then serve as precedents for future breaches—of future expansion. Be careful what you ask for!

O. Hamilton returns to the main theme of the limited delegation of authority to the federal government (No. 32): *"But as the plan of the convention aims only at a partial union or consolidation, the State governments would clearly retain all the rights of sovereignty which they before had, and which were not, by that act, Exclusively delegated to the United States."* Hamilton's main point is the convention had taken "the most pointed care" to ensure the powers "not explicitly divested in favor of the Union" remain "in full vigor" with the states.

P. The doctrine of enumerated powers is discussed throughout the *Federalist Papers,* but Madison's discussion of three of those powers is especially important in light of developments in the twentieth century that have vastly expanded their scope. After reviewing the main areas over which the federal government would have power, he answers objections that were raised about the first of Congress's enumerated powers: the power to tax "to provide for the common Defense and general Welfare of the United States." That wording, skeptics charged, would allow the government virtually unlimited power toward those ends. Madison answers:

> *Had no other enumeration or definition of the powers of the Congress been found in the Constitution, than the general expressions just cited, the authors of the objection might have had some color for it. ... But what color [merit] can the objection have, when a specification of the objects alluded to by these general terms immediately follows, and is not even separated by a longer pause than*

a semicolon? ... Nothing is more natural nor common than first to use a general phrase, and then to explain and qualify it by a recital of particulars. (No. 41)

In other words, the terms "common Defense" and "general Welfare" are simply general headings. It is in the enumerated powers that follow where Congress finds the objects over which it has authority—and for which it may tax.

    Q. In a similar way, Madison addresses the function of Congress's power to regulate "Commerce among the States," saying without that power,

the great and essential power of regulating foreign commerce would have been incomplete and ineffectual. A very material object of this power was the relief of the States which import and export through other States, from the improper contributions levied on them by the latter. (No. 42)

Thus, the commerce power was granted to ensure robust commerce—free especially from interference by the states. It was not, as it has become today, a power to regulate anything and everything for any reason whatsoever.

    R. Finally, Madison answers those who had objected to the last of Congress's eighteen enumerated powers—the power "to make all laws which shall be necessary and proper for carrying into execution the foregoing powers, and all other powers vested by this Constitution in the government of the United States, or in any department or officer thereof." It would have been impossible, he writes, to have attempted "a complete digest of laws on every subject to which the Constitution relates." And what if Congress should misconstrue this or any other of its powers?

In the first instance, the success of the usurpation will depend on the executive and judiciary departments, which are to expound and give effect to the legislative acts; and in the last resort a remedy must be obtained from the people, who can, by the election of more faithful representatives, annul the acts of the usurpers. (No. 44)

Madison is confident the citizens of the nation will see to it that Congress does not exceed its delegated and enumerated powers.

S. And so in the *Federalist Papers*, as in the Declaration and the Constitution, we see the extraordinary thought and care that went into America's Founding. The doctrine of enumerated powers was central to the Framers' design. It granted the federal government enough power to discharge its responsibilities, but not so much as to threaten our liberty. But it is up to us, to each generation, to see to it that our officials are faithful to the principles the Framers secured through that extraordinary thought and care.

4

Distributing the Mass of Power among its Constituent Parts

Separation of Powers in the *Federalist Papers*

by John Shu

Federalist Papers referenced in essay: *#47, 48, 51*

A. The authors of the *Federalist Papers* supported dividing the national government's power amongst three separate, co-equal branches of government: the legislature, the executive, and the judiciary. The proposed constitution further separated the legislature into two sub-branches, the House of Representatives and the Senate, in order to guarantee the legislature did not become too powerful, and minimize the possibility of tyranny by majority.

B. In the *Federalist Papers,* we encounter specific mention of "checks and balances" as a way to restrict government power and prevent government from consolidating and/or abusing its power. The proposed constitution essentially organized the governmental system so each branch of government had its own distinctive powers and was able to block certain acts of the other two branches, and yet simultaneously be co-dependent on the other two branches to operate.

C. In No. 47, Madison examines *"the particular structure of this government, and the distribution of this mass of power among its constituent parts."* His goal was to explain the proposed U.S. Constitution's separation of powers among the executive, legislative, and judicial branches of government. The genius of separating power and duties among three different branches of government is that in doing so it simultaneously accommodates and takes advantage of man's natural tendencies to act out of self-interest.

D. Many influential people worried, with respect to separation of powers, the proposed U.S. Constitution did not go *far enough* in separating powers amongst the different branches of government. Many of the former colonists still had all-too fresh and painful memories, earned in blood and sacrifice, of the Revolutionary War. The last thing the former colonists wanted was to create something that could become another form of tyrannical government. The *Federalist Papers* attempted to calm those fears and rally support to ratify the proposed constitution.

E. In No. 47, Madison directly reached out to those concerned that the proposed constitution did not go sufficiently far in separating the powers amongst the executive, legislative, and judicial branches. Madison began by affirming his genuine belief in the vital importance of separating powers, and the principle of separation of powers was uncontroversial and inviolate. Madison wrote *"accumulation of all powers, legislative, executive, and judiciary, in the same hands ... may justly be pronounced the very definition of tyranny."*

F. Another commonly expressed concern was the proposed constitution did not contain specific language clearly separating government powers amongst the three branches of government. Madison's key response was a specific constitutional declaration of the separation of powers was neither necessary nor a reliable safeguard against tyranny. Madison further argued that complete separation among the branches was neither necessary nor feasible. He acknowledged the proposed constitution *intentionally* intertwined the three branches and simultaneously made them separate and co-dependent on each other.

G. Madison asserted this structure did not violate the principle of separation of powers. He cited Montesquieu, a French philosopher, who argued tyranny results when one branch of government simultaneously holds the powers of another branch. Madison, however, argues that Montesquieu *"did not mean that these departments ought to have no PARTIAL AGENCY in, or CONTROL over, the acts of each other* (No. 47).*"* The most important elements of separation of powers are (1) no branch exercises all the powers of another; (2) there be security of each branch against the others; and (3) the proposed constitution contained those elements. Completely separating the branches of government such that they have no interaction with each other is a practical impossibility.

H. Madison analyzed the individual constitutions of several states to enlist support for ratification and to bolster his argument that absolute separation of powers was not ideal and impractical. Madison wrote even though certain states had specific "separation of powers" language in their constitutions, *"there is not a single instance in which the several departments of power have been kept absolutely separate and distinct* (No. 47).*"* Many states had constitutions which contained language clearly separating the executive, legislative, and judicial branches. Madison notes, however, *"the legislative, executive, and judiciary departments have not been kept totally separate and distinct"* and in fact were intertwined. Madison's point was if the several states did not think their own constitutions did not violate the principle of separation of powers, then neither did the proposed U.S. Constitution.

I. Madison continues his separation of powers discussion in No. 48 where he again reaches out to critics and skeptics of the proposed constitution. Many were concerned that too much power might reside in the legislative branch, and it would be too easy for the legislature to assume executive and judiciary powers without effective opposition from those branches. One could reasonably argue that the legislature is the branch which is most likely to abuse power because the proposed constitution granted it a degree of greater power compared to the other two branches, such as the power of the purse, the power to declare war, and the power to regulate commerce amongst the states.

J. The arguments in No. 48 demonstrate Madison's sensitivity to potential legislative tyranny, and shows the proposed constitution would prevent it. Madison was wise enough to realize that writing down each branch's power boundaries is insufficient. He noted,

> *the conclusion which I am warranted in drawing from these observations is, that a mere demarcation on parchment of the constitutional limits of the several departments, is not a sufficient guard against those encroachments which lead to a tyrannical concentration of all the powers of government in the same hands.* (No. 48)

K. Madison explained the structural differences amongst the legislature's, executive's and judiciary's powers. The proposed constitution intentionally provided structural overlap in the defined powers assigned to each of the three government branches.

L. In No. 51, Madison first uses the specific term "checks and balances," a common term today. The *Papers* largely deal with the allocation of national power, preventing any one branch of government from becoming too powerful, and protecting individual citizens from abuses of power. *Federalist* No. 51 shows the Framers of the proposed constitution intentionally designed a government that (1) would protect the citizens from tyranny, (2) would most likely succeed at their long-term goals for the young republic, (3) would be intentionally inefficient at times, and (4) would do this while taking advantage of, instead of fighting against, man's inherent selfish and self-protective nature. Madison again stresses his belief that each branch should be largely independent from the other while also arguing absolute separation of the branches was not only impossible, but harmful.

M. Madison argued the proposed constitution would protect the people from oppression of the majority and also oppression of the minority. Madison supported dividing the national government in a way such that each branch in and of itself would be a type of safeguard against tyranny. Because each branch of government was simultaneously separate and interdependent, it had to work together with the other branches in order to achieve the goals of national government. Moreover, to reign in the power of the legislature, the Framers separated the legislature into two sub-parts, independent and interdependent on each other; they bolstered the executive's power by giving veto power over legislation; and they provided the legislature a counterweight to override the veto through a supermajority.

N. The constitutional structures that are an important part of checks and balances and conducive to a just government are as follows:

Legislative Branch (Article I)
- Checks the Executive Branch through
  - impeachment power (House of Representatives)
  - trial of impeachments (Senate)
  - selection of President (House) and Vice President (Senate) if no majority of electoral votes

- override of presidential veto
- advice and consent on executive appointments (Senate)
- power to tax and spend
- power to raise armies
- power to declare war
- the president must, from time to time, give Congress information about the state of the union

- Checks the Judicial Branch through
  - advice and consent of judicial nominees (Senate)
  - impeachment power (House)
  - trial of impeachments (Senate)
  - power to start constitutional amendment process
  - power to set courts inferior to the Supreme Court
  - power to set jurisdiction of courts
  - power to set the size of the Supreme Court

Executive Branch (Article II)

- Checks the Legislature through
  - veto power
  - Vice President serves as president of the Senate and provides tie-breaking vote
  - executive is commander in chief of the military
  - may provide recess appointments
  - may call one or both houses of the Legislature into session, in case of emergency
  - may force adjournment when both houses cannot agree on adjournment

- o executive's compensation may not be diminished

- Checks the Judiciary through
  - o power to appoint federal judges
  - o pardon power

Judicial Branch (Article III)

- Checks the Legislature through
  - o judicial review of laws
  - o lifetime appointment of judges assuming "good behavior"
  - o judges' compensation may not be diminished by Congress
- Checks the Executive through
  - o judicial review
  - o chief justice of the United States presides over a Senate trial regarding presidential impeachment

O. Madison believed the Constitution, in both its explicit structure and its implicit assumptions about human nature, would ensure the ultimate goal of government: justice. *"It is the end of civil society. It ever has been and ever will be pursued until it be obtained, or until liberty be lost in the pursuit* (No. 51)."

5

The Proposed Constitution ... Is Neither Wholly Federal nor Wholly National

Federalism in the *Federalist Papers*

by John Shu

Federalist Papers referenced in essay: #9, 33, 39, 44, 45, 63, 68

A. Every American citizen has a type of dual citizenship. Americans are citizens of the United States, and may carry a U.S. passport, but Americans are also citizens of the respective states in which they live, and may carry that state's "passport," such as a driver's license or state identity card. A person may be criminally charged for what appears to be the same criminal act in both state court and federal court. This does not violate the Fifth Amendment protection against double-jeopardy because state and federal governments are considered separate political entities. The principle of federalism allows both of these scenarios.

B. Federalism is the division of governmental powers amongst the various levels of governments: national, state, and sometimes local. Federalism is a crucial principle in the U.S. Constitution, yet the Constitution never uses the actual word. Our modern-day government system has several basic federal characteristics: (1) legally distinct governmental domains (*e.g.,* national and state government); (2) the states have certain powers and the federal government has certain powers, but the states are subordinate to the national government and the U.S. Constitution is the supreme law of the land; (3) the states have a general "police power" to regulate behavior and enforce order within their own borders for the betterment of their citizens' general welfare, morals, health, and safety; whereas the federal government's authority comes from its powers which are specifically enumerated in the Constitution; and (4) the U.S. Supreme Court is the final arbiter of legal conflicts between states, as well as between a state and the national government.

C. The federalist nature of our government came about as a result of hard-won lessons. The Founders feared the tyranny of a powerful national executive like King George III, but the Articles of Confederation, fully ratified on March 1, 1781, were not working. One reason was because the states had too much sovereign power. For example, certain states issued their own paper money after the Revolutionary War, which caused runaway inflation. Thus, it was important that only the national government could mint and issue currency. The precarious financial situation of the young nation led to discontent and even armed rebellion. This troubled George Washington, who wrote, *"Let us have a government by which our lives, liberties, and properties will be secured, or let us know the worst at once."* James Madison, also convinced that the young nation needed a stronger national government, among other things, to prevent states from infringing on citizens' rights, wrote *"liberty may be endangered by the abuses of liberty as well as the abuses of power* (No. 63)." He and other Founders looked to the principle of federalism to create the proper balance between national and state power.

D. In light of these challenges, the Founders had particular goals when developing the U.S. Constitution, such as: (1) a government responsive to its citizens; (2) a political system that enhanced, rather than discouraged, interaction between government and its citizens; (3) a political system that allowed for a peaceful coexistence of political order, social order, and individual liberties; and (4) a judicial system that was fair in ensuring justice and not beholden to either the legislature or the executive.

E. The *Federalist Papers* contains numerous passages that address federalism and its role in the proposed U.S. Constitution. For example, Hamilton argues in No. 9 that creating both a sovereign national government and sovereign state governments subordinate to the national government would help protect individual rights against potential abuses by both the national and state governments. Madison expresses concerns over these potential abuses, particularly his fear of the *"tyranny of the majority,"* as opposed to *"tyranny of the minority,"* especially at the state level. However, Madison in No. 45 wrote the "*State governments may be regarded as constituent and essential parts of the federal government*" and the "*component parts of the State governments will in no instance be indebted for their appointment to the direct agency of the federal government.*" At the same time, Madison noted insufficient federal power would be problematic. The Articles of Confederation had failed in part because the several states had veto power over each other, causing the national government to be weak, thus preventing the nation from efficiently governing and operating.

F. Our system of government, unlike a confederation, does not permit the individual states to be equal in sovereignty to the national government. As George Washington envisioned, the United States of America is a *union* of states, not a *confederacy* of states. Article VI, Clause 2 of the U.S. Constitution is known as the "Supremacy Clause" because it establishes the U.S. Constitution, U.S. treaties, and federal statutes as "the supreme law of the land." Alexander Hamilton in No. 33 stated the Supremacy Clause is important so the national government could properly execute its powers. National laws would have no "teeth" if they were not considered supreme. James Madison also emphasizes the critical need to have supreme federal law; otherwise, our system of government would be *"an inversion of the fundamental principles of all government; it would have seen the authority of the whole society every where"* meaning the national government *"subordinate to the authority of the parts"* meaning the separate state governments; *"it would have seen a monster, in which the head was under the direction of the members [limbs]* (No. 44)."

G. Madison, in No. 39, explains how the national government is to be both state-based (*e.g.,* two senators from each state, regardless of a state's population) and population-based (number of congressmen from a particular state based on that state's population). In order to avoid the tyranny of the majority, the several states were to originally ratify the Constitution and later to amend it. The process of amending the Constitution may begin at either the federal level, where two-thirds of both houses of Congress may vote to propose a constitutional amendment, or at the state level, where two-thirds of the state legislatures may ask Congress to call a national convention to propose a constitutional amendment. Ratification of a proposed constitutional amendment requires at least three-fourths of the state legislatures or ratifying conventions in three-fourths of the states. Thus, much of the power of the federal government comes from, and relies on, the several states.

H. Madison also explains powers held by the federal government, and exercised by the Congress, are also derived both from the states and the people within the states. The House of Representatives derives its powers directly from the people, because the people directly elected their representatives and the number of representatives of each state is based on population. The Senate originally derived its powers from the states, because the state legislatures chose their senators (until the Seventeenth Amendment in 1913 provided for direct election of senators). Each state has two Senators regardless of geographic or population size.

I. The election of the president, according to the original constitution, is also based upon the principle of federalism, in this case a mix of population-based and state-based power. Each state has a number of electors equal to the number of representatives (*i.e.,* a measure of the state's population) plus the number of senators (every state in the nation, regardless of population, has two senators.) The Electoral College is an indirect election in which

> *the electors, chosen in each State, are to assemble and vote in the State in which they are chosen, this detached and divided situation will expose them much less to heats and ferments, that might be communicated from them to the people, than if they were all to be convened at one time, in one place.* (No. 68)

J. This system addressed concerns regarding the preservation of state sovereignty. As long as federal power was exercised by a president who was elected by representatives and senators accountable to the states as well as the citizens of the states, state sovereignty and individual liberty would be preserved. Moreover, Hamilton confidently predicted this mixture of state-based and national constituencies would ensure that *"the office of President will never fall to the lot of any man who is not in an eminent degree endowed with the requisite qualifications* (No. 68)."

K. In the years since the Founding, many Americans have thought of the states as "laboratories" where, because of their sovereignty within their own borders, they could experiment without necessarily affecting their sister states or the nation. In the 1932 case of *New State Ice Company v. Liebmann*, Associate

Supreme Court Justice Louis Brandeis wrote in his dissent, "*It is one of the happy incidents of the federal system that a single courageous State may, if its citizens choose, serve as a laboratory; and try novel social and economic experiments without risk to the rest of the country.*" In the 2005 case of *Gonzales v. Raich*, Associate Supreme Court Justice Sandra Day O'Connor wrote in her dissent that

> *this case exemplifies the role of States as laboratories. The States' core police powers have always included authority to define criminal law and to protect the health, safety and welfare of their citizens ... Exercising those powers, California (by ballot initiative and then by legislative codification) has come to its own conclusion about the difficult and sensitive question of whether marijuana should be available to relieve pain and suffering.*

L. The states continue to have great power under the Constitution. As Madison wrote, "*the powers delegated by the proposed Constitution to the Federal government are few and defined. Those which are to remain in the State governments are numerous and indefinite* (No. 45)." The Tenth and Eleventh Amendments also reflect state sovereignty and federalism.

M. Federalism, which divides power among the federal and state governments and the people, is an integral part of our system of government. Part of the genius of our Constitution is as Madison cleverly explained,

> *the proposed Constitution, therefore, is, in strictness, neither a national nor a federal Constitution, but a composition of both. In its foundation it is federal, not national; in the sources from which the ordinary powers of the government are drawn, it is partly federal and*

partly national; in the operation of these powers, it is national, not federal; in the extent of them, again, it is federal, not national; and finally, in the authoritative mode of introducing amendments, it is neither wholly federal nor wholly national. (No. 39)

6

The Judiciary has Neither Force nor Will, but Merely Judgment

The Independent Judiciary

by John Shu

Federalist Papers referenced in essay: #27, 78, 79, 81

A. As Alexander Hamilton wrote in *Federalist* No. 78, *"WE PROCEED now to an examination of the judiciary department of the proposed government."*

B. The U.S. Constitution does not contain much text about the U.S. Supreme Court or any other federal court. Article III is the shortest of the first three articles, and only the first two sections of Article III cover the judiciary's structure, even though the judiciary is the third and co-equal branch of our national government. Federal judges— those nominated and confirmed under Article III— are responsible for interpreting the law and the U.S. Constitution. The U.S. Supreme Court is the highest court in the land, but the Constitution only specifically mentions the chief justice in Article II, not Article III — and that is with respect to presidential impeachment. The Constitution does not even specifically mandate the size of the U.S. Supreme Court, which currently has eight associate justices and one chief justice. In the past the number of Supreme Court justices has fluctuated from as few as five to as many as ten. Some constitutional scholars believe the framers of the proposed constitution put the judiciary in Article

III because it was to be the weakest of the three branches, although in some ways the federal judiciary has enormous authority and power.

C. The Constitution does not mandate age, residency, or citizenship requirements for federal judges as it does for elected officials. In fact, the Constitution does not even specifically mandate a federal judge need be a lawyer, although practically speaking it probably would be best for a judge to first have been a lawyer. While all Supreme Court justices were lawyers, not all previously served as judges.

D. The U.S. Constitution requires the president of the United States to nominate judicial candidates, and the Senate, through its "advice and consent" role, confirms or rejects them. Once confirmed, federal judges have lifetime tenure during "good behavior" and their salaries "shall not be diminished during their continuance in office." The House of Representatives may impeach a judge, and if impeached, the Senate would preside over the trial.

E. Article III courts consist entirely of certain federal courts, namely the United States Supreme Court and the "inferior courts" that Congress established as Article III courts, currently composed of the thirteen U.S. Courts of Appeals, the ninety-four U.S. District Courts, and the U.S. Court of International Trade. The U.S. Supreme Court has original jurisdiction "in all Cases affecting Ambassadors, other public Ministers and Consuls, and those in which a State shall be Party" (Article III, Section 2, Clause 2 of the U.S. Constitution).

F. Alexander Hamilton wrote the *Federalist Papers* about the judicial branch. In them, he discussed the importance of an independent judiciary and of constitutional supremacy. In Hamilton's view, federal judges are the *"faithful guardians"* of the "*rights of the Constitution, and of individuals* (No. 78)." Hamilton also viewed the Constitution as the fundamental law which is supreme to any legislative statute and the most accurate expression of the people's will. "*[The Constitution] will become the SUPREME LAW of the land; to the observance of which all officers, legislative, executive, and judicial in each State, will be bound by the sanctity of an oath* (No. 27).*"

G. Hamilton discusses the judiciary's place in government and the importance of judges being financially independent from both the executive and legislative branches, which would insulate them from pressure from the executive branch, the legislative branch, or the popular vote. This is why the Constitution, in Article III, Section 1, states, "The Judges, both of the supreme and inferior Courts, shall hold their Offices during good Behaviour, and shall, at stated Times, receive for their Services, a Compensation, which shall not be diminished during their Continuance in Office." Thus, a federal judge's salary may not be reduced as long as he or she is in office, and federal judges hold their jobs for life, assuming "good Behaviour." The House of Representatives may impeach a federal judge, and when that happens the Senate oversees the trial.

H. As Hamilton puts it, using "good behavior" is the correct standard to use for judicial tenure because

> *[t]he standard of good behavior for the continuance in office of the judicial magistracy, is certainly one of the most valuable of the modern improvements in the practice of government. In a monarchy it is an excellent barrier to the despotism of the prince; in a republic it is a no less excellent barrier to the encroachments and oppressions of the representative body. And it is the best expedient which can be devised in any government, to secure a steady, upright, and impartial administration of the laws.* (No.

78)

Hamilton also explains why judges with lifetime tenure must be financially independent of the executive and legislative branches so they can do their jobs without undue influence. Hamilton notes that, next to lifetime tenure,

> *nothing can contribute more to independence of the judges than a fixed provision for their support .... In the general course of human nature, A POWER OVER A MAN's SUBSISTENCE AMOUNTS TO A POWER OVER HIS WILL. And we can never hope to see realized in practice, the complete separation of the judicial from the legislative power, in any system which leaves the former dependent for pecuniary resources on the occasional grants of the latter.* (No. 79)

Thus, Congress can increase the judges' salaries but never reduce them.

I. Forcibly removing a federal judge from office is as difficult as removing a president, perhaps even more so, requiring the House of Representatives to impeach the judge and the Senate to try and convict the judge. Combining lifetime tenure, financial security, and the difficulty of removing a judge at whim allows judges to be insulated from pressures of the executive and legislative branches. They are also freed from the pressures of popular politics, which is sometimes described as tyranny of the majority. Hamilton believed that an independent judiciary would protect the rights of individuals when threatened by the majority. Hamilton and the other Framers were astute enough to see that having an impartial judiciary to prevent the other two branches from passing and executing laws that harm individual liberties or harmed the constitutionally safeguarded republican government, was essential. The independent judiciary is free to preserve the liberty of citizens and states.

J. Hamilton also noted that judges should have lifetime tenure because no one could predict or reliably say at what age a judge could no longer serve. Moreover, some laws or decisions require several years before their full meaning and effect can be appreciated. A short or unsure term of judicial office would likely discourage talented and honest people from accepting an appointment to the Article III courts because, for example, they would be reluctant to give up lucrative private law practices to accept a temporary or short-term judicial appointment.

K. In No. 78, Hamilton wrote if *"the courts of justice are to be considered as the bulwarks of a limited Constitution against legislative encroachments"* lifetime tenure for federal judges is essential for the *"independent spirit in the judges which must be essential to the faithful performance of so arduous a duty."* Hamilton noted many states already had constitutions where their respective judiciaries were distinct and independent bodies, not part of the legislature. An independent judiciary also shields the courts from factionalism within Congress, so that, as Hamilton puts it, there would be less *"reason to fear that the pestilential breath of faction may poison the fountains of justice* (No. 81)."

L. In Hamilton's view, judges are required to void legislative and executive acts that are contrary to the Constitution. He noted an independent judiciary protects individual rights from the executive branch as well as from the legislative branch. Without the judiciary, Hamilton wrote *"all the reservations of particular rights or privileges would amount to nothing* (No. 78)." Hamilton saw the courts to be an intermediary between the people and the other two branches so, among other things, the courts could keep the other branches within their constitutional limits. As Hamilton wrote, *"The interpretation of the laws is the proper and peculiar* *province of the courts* (No. 78)."

M. In Hamilton's view, the courts are responsible for determining what a law means, or interpreting the law. Hamilton believed federal judges may not "legislate from the bench," meaning they may not substitute their own policy or political preferences for the legislature's. As Hamilton wrote in No. 78, *"The courts must declare the sense of the law; and if they should be disposed to exercise WILL instead of JUDGEMENT, the consequence would equally be the substitution of their pleasure to that of the legislative body."* Thus, Congress passes legislation, and the president either signs or vetoes it, usually in response to constituents' demands. The judges are to interpret the laws, apply those laws to the particular facts in the litigation, and decide whether the laws are constitutional.

N. In the Framers' eyes, judges were not to be affected by popular will, unless directly expressed in the Constitution itself. In Hamilton's view, this meant the judiciary was the branch most closely tied to the Constitution, which is both a recipient and source of superior law. Hamilton also notes, however, *"By a limited Constitution, I understand one which contains specific exceptions to the legislative authority* (No. 78)." Hamilton's use of the term "limited" instead of "limiting" suggests he viewed certain principles that secure individual rights and the protection of the states, along with certain restrictions on the government branches, limited by the Constitution itself.

O. The Constitution neither explicitly grants nor forbids the power of judicial review, which is the power of the federal courts to rule on the constitutionality of laws. The *Federalist Papers*, however, discuss judicial review. For example, in No. 78, Hamilton wrote the federal courts have a duty to *"declare all acts contrary to the manifest tenor of the constitution void."* Hamilton further discusses judicial review in No. 80, writing that *"there ought always to be a constitutional method of giving efficacy to constitutional provisions .... This power must either be a direct negative on the State laws, or an authority in the federal courts to overrule such as might be in manifest contravention of the articles of Union [i.e., the Constitution]."* Because the proposed constitution did not grant the national government the power to veto state laws, Hamilton believed the federal courts had the power to determine the constitutionality of law.

P. *Marbury v. Madison* (1803) was the first time the U.S. Supreme Court invalidated a federal law by declaring it unconstitutional. Chief Justice John Marshall's decision established the court's right of judicial review under Article III of the Constitution.

Q. *Marbury* is important because the protections and limitations that the Constitution imposes on Congress and the president would be ineffective if the courts did not have the power to declare laws unconstitutional. Hamilton recognizes in No. 81 that critics of the proposed constitution feared the Supreme Court's authority would be greater than the legislature's, especially because the Court's *"decisions will not be in any manner subject to the revision or correction of the legislative body."* This concern still exists today. Hamilton responds to the critics by noting the legislature has the power of confirmation, or "advice and consent," in the selection of judges, and also has the power of impeachment and conviction to remove judges from their offices.

R. Hamilton never viewed the judiciary as "superior" to the legislature. Hamilton's view was the Constitution was the ultimate expression of the people, and thus *"the Constitution ought to be preferred to the statute, the intention of the people to the intention of their agents* (No. 78)." Hamilton believed the judiciary, by interpreting the laws, would protect the people by preventing the legislature from overreaching or exceeding its constitutional powers and encroaching upon individual rights.

S. Hamilton foresaw *"particular misconstructions and contraventions of the will of the legislature may now and again happen; but they can never be so extensive as to amount to an inconvenience, or in any sensible degree to affect the order of the political system* (No. 81)." Hamilton viewed the legislature's power of impeachment as a significant deterrent against judges usurping their authority, along with the judiciary's *"comparative weakness, and from its total incapacity to support its usurpations by force* (No. 81)."

T. Hamilton, then, viewed the judiciary as the "weakest of the three departments of power" and

the judiciary, from the nature of its functions, will always be the least dangerous to the political rights of the Constitution ... The Executive not only dispenses the honors, but holds the sword of the community. The legislature not only commands the purse, but prescribes the rules by which the duties and rights of every citizen are to be regulated. The judiciary, on the contrary, has no influence over either the sword or the purse; no direction either of the strength or of the wealth of the society; and can take no active resolution whatever. It may truly be said to have neither FORCE nor WILL, but merely judgment; and must ultimately depend upon the aid of the executive arm even for the efficacy of its judgments. (No. 78)

U. Throughout American history, the judiciary has been both ignored and supported by the other two branches, as well as the states. In 1832, President Andrew Jackson, upset at the Supreme

Court's decision in *Worcester v. Georgia*, reportedly said "[Chief Justice] John Marshall has made his decision, now let him enforce it!" Of course, Marshall had no way of enforcing his decision and Jackson won the day. After the Supreme Court decided the landmark case of *Brown v. Board of Education* of Topeka in 1954, which struck down segregation, several southern governors refused to desegregate their state's schools. Eventually, Presidents Dwight D. Eisenhower and John F. Kennedy used the threat of military action to enforce the judiciary's decisions and orders.

V. Although the debate continues over the role and reach of the judicial branch, in general, most would agree the federal judiciary remains the guardian of the Constitution, and ideally interprets laws with a view towards preserving the Constitution for future generations.

7

To Make Their Interests Coincide With Their Duty

How the Constitution Leads Public Officials to Make Good Decisions

by Robert T. Miller

Federalist Papers referenced in essay: #1, 3, 6, 10, 15, 39, 51, 57, 68, 72, 84

A. "*The true test of a good government is its aptitude and tendency to produce a good administration* (No. 68)." Like every sentence in the *Federalist Papers*, this needs to be read carefully. You may think Hamilton means a *good government* is one in which public officials make wise and prudent decisions—that is, produces what he calls a *good administration*. If that is what you think, you missed his point. An absolute dictator may make wise and prudent decisions, if he happens to be wise and prudent and possesses a particularly virtuous character. The Roman emperor Marcus Aurelius was perhaps such a ruler. Human experience, which Hamilton calls the "*best oracle of wisdom*" (No. 15), has shown that dictators tend to be quite the opposite, inflicting misery and ruin on the peoples they rule. The possibility of good dictators doesn't make dictatorship a good form of government. Hamilton does not mean a good government is one in which the rulers make good decisions; he means something more complicated. He implies a good government has an internal organization—a constitution— that tends to cause public officials to make good decisions.

51

B. A constitution that tends to cause public officials to make good decisions sounds simple. As Madison says:

> *The aim of every political constitution is, or ought to be,*
> *first to obtain for rulers men who possess most wisdom to*
> *discern, and most virtue to pursue, the common good of*
> *the society; and in the next place, to take the most*
> *effectual precautions for keeping them virtuous whilst*
> *they continue to hold the public trust.* (No. 57)

Like so many things, however, devising such a constitution is easier said than done. The brilliance of the American Constitution—the reason it has survived so long and been copied so often, becoming a model to the world—is that it largely solved this problem. It creates a system of procedures for selecting public officials and ordering how they make decisions that are in the best interests of society. How does it do that?

C. To answer that question, it helps to take a step back and see what the Founders thought about the origins and purposes of government and about human nature. In No. 15, Hamilton asks, *"Why has government been instituted at all? Because the passions of men will not conform to the dictates of reason and justice, without constraint."* In other words, if not controlled by a superior force, people will violate the rights of others. As the Declaration of Independence says, "To secure these rights, Governments are instituted among Men." That means a government, if it is to fulfill its essential function, must be powerful enough to protect its citizens against threats to their rights and interests, whether from foreign nations or homegrown wrongdoers. The constitution created by the Articles of Confederation proved far too weak in this regard, and was one reason the Framers met in Philadelphia in 1787—to propose to the American people changes that would make the federal government more powerful.

D. We need a government powerful enough to protect our rights. Solving this problem, however, immediately creates another and potentially even worse issue. For, as Madison famously puts it, *"If men were angels, no government would be necessary. If angels were to govern men, neither external nor internal controls on government would be necessary* (No. 51)." That is, if everyone always acted fairly and reasonably, there would be no wrongdoers for government to restrain, and so government would be unnecessary. Furthermore, if public officials always acted fairly and reasonably, the form of government would not matter, since such morally perfect government officials would never misuse the power of government. But humans do not always act fairly and reasonably. In fact, *"men are ambitious, vindictive, and rapacious"* (No. 6), and they often act out of pride, jealousy, greed, rage, sentiment, partisanship, and the love of power. This is as true of people chosen to be public officials as of any others. Hence, it is a dangerous thing to entrust humans with the power of government, for they can use the very powers granted to protect the rights of citizens to violate those rights. Madison continues,

> *In framing a government which is to be administered by men over men, the great difficulty lies in this: you must first enable the government to control the governed; and in the next place oblige it to control itself.* (No. 51)

E. You may think it is easy to prevent government officials from misusing their power. All you have to do is include in the constitution a bill of rights: a list of rights that the government may not violate. Our Constitution, as it currently exists, includes a bill of rights in its first ten amendments, but the original document drafted in Philadelphia in 1787 did not. The authors of the *Federalist* thought it was actually better that way (No. 84). This was not because they thought such rights were unimportant; on the contrary, they were extremely zealous to protect them. They thought the mere recitation of such rights in a bill was not an effective method of protecting them. Hamilton wrote that security for our rights, *"whatever fine declarations may be inserted in any constitution respecting it, must altogether depend on public opinion, and on the general spirit of the people and of the government,"* which is *"the only solid basis of all our rights* (No. 84)." If there is a strong enough desire among the people and their public officials to violate someone's rights, then a bill of rights protecting those rights is a mere *"parchment barrier* (No. 48)" and the government will violate the right, nonetheless.

F. Experience has largely confirmed this view. In *Plessy v. Ferguson* (1896), the Supreme Court held, without violating the Equal Protection Clause of the Fourteenth Amendment, a state could maintain "separate but equal" public facilities for black citizens and white citizens—a view that it would later reject in *Brown v. Board of Education* (1954). What changed between 1896 and 1954? Not the text of the Fourteenth Amendment— it is exactly the same. What changed was "public opinion" and "the general spirit of the people and of government," which had come to regard racial discrimination as gravely unjust. What good were words on paper without individual citizens to remind us of them; without judges on the Supreme Court inclined to enforce them; without a man like President Eisenhower willing to use federal troops to carry the court's decision into effect; and, most important of all, without an American public who, for the most part, supported President Eisenhower's decision?

G. In the view of the Framers, the true safeguard of the rights of the people are not enumerations of these rights on paper, but systems of government that empower individuals inclined to respect them. And this brings us to our original problem: how do we organize government so the procedures whereby public officials are selected and their decisions will tend to result in decisions that benefit the public? The answer to this question is one of the great insights embodied in the Constitution and explained in the *Federalist Papers*. As Hamilton puts it: *"The best security for the fidelity of mankind is to make their interests coincide with their duty* (No. 72)." In other words, given that humans are generally self-interested (and often ambitious, greedy, vain, and jealous), we should use these motives to protect the public interest by cleverly arranging the internal structure of the government so office holders will find it in their *self*-interest to make decisions that promote the *public* interest.

H. The first means of accomplishing this arises from the most basic structure of the government—that is, from its being a republic. *"We may define a republic,"* Madison writes, *"to be ... a government which derives all its powers directly or indirectly from the great body of the people"* and

> *[i]t is Sufficient for such a government that the persons administering it be appointed, either directly or indirectly, by the people; and that they hold their appointments"* either *"during pleasure, for a limited period, or during good behavior.* (No. 39)

Public officials must have, Madison suggests, *"a dependence on the people* (No. 51)." The public officials must obtain, and retain, their offices only if the people generally are satisfied with them. Public officials must periodically stand for election and re-election, as do our senators, representatives, and presidents (in Madison's terms, "direct" appointment by the people); or must be appointed or removed by such officials, as our cabinet secretaries, heads of administrative agencies, and judges (in Madison's terms, "indirect" appointment by the people).

I. This idea seems simple, but it comes with important assumptions. Since we want public officials to make decisions that benefit not just one class or group of people, but the public interest generally, it is essential the ultimate power to choose officials comes from *"the great body of society, not from an inconsiderable proportion, or a favored class of it* (No. 39)." If only one class of person determined who the public officials would be, we could expect public officials to make decisions favoring people in that class, not benefiting society as a whole.

J. Furthermore, it is easy to see how, if public officials depend on the people for getting and retaining office, they have an incentive to do what the people want. However, this is not the same as saying they have an incentive to do what's in the public interest—what really contributes to the good of society. Thus, Jay writes, *"the people of any country (if, like the Americans, intelligent and well-informed) seldom adopt and steadily persevere for many years in an erroneous opinion respecting their interests* (No. 3)." It is a fundamental presupposition of the Constitution that, by and large, the American people are intelligent and informed enough to be the best judges of what is in their own interest.

K. That idea may sound trivial, but it has profound implications. For instance, some people think wealthy individuals, big corporations, and powerful unions are able to "buy" election results by tricking a majority of the people into electing representatives who will advance the financier's interests instead of the public's. These concerns may lead to calls for campaign finance reform, but the Framers would have had none of this. Madison asks,

> *What are we to say to the men who profess the most flaming zeal for republican government, yet boldly impeach the fundamental principle of it; who pretend to be champions for the right and the capacity of the people*

to choose their own rulers, yet maintain that they will prefer those only who will immediately and infallibly betray the trust committed to them? (No. 57)

For the Framers, faith in the good sense of the people is the ultimate safeguard of liberty.

L. Although "*a dependence on the people is, no doubt, the primary control on government,*" nevertheless "*experience has taught mankind the necessity of auxiliary precautions* (No. 51)." How so? By creating within the same government "*opposite and rival interests*" so "*the constant aim is to divide and arrange the several offices in such a manner as that each may be a check on the other that the private interest of every individual may be sentinel over the public rights* (No. 51)." This is the famous system of checks and balances. In this system, before the government can act, the Constitution generally requires the concurrence of many public officials, so, if some are embarking on a course of action that might benefit some people, but is nevertheless detrimental to the public interest, other officials will have an incentive to oppose or stop that action, alerting the public to the danger and hoping thereby to capture the goodwill of the public. Since all public officials are dependent, directly or indirectly, on the will of the people, if a measure is contrary to the best interests of the whole, any public official who exposes the measure as such is likely to be rewarded by the people, either by being retained in office or even promoted to higher office. Thus, the system makes "*their interest coincide with their duty* (No. 72)."

M. The legislative process is an obvious example of this principle. One of the most important functions of government is to make laws, and under the Constitution, all three branches of government must, in one way or another, agree in order to pass the law. Congress must pass the law, but, since the legislative branch is the most powerful branch of government, the Constitution intentionally weakens it by dividing it into two houses and requiring the concurrence of both to make a law. The purpose of this is *"to render them, by different modes of election and different principles of action, as little connected with each other as the nature of their common functions and their common dependence on society will admit* (No. 51)." So, if a law is popular in a large number of states, but not in states accounting for a majority of the population, it may pass in the Senate, but likely fail in the House of Representatives. Similarly, if a law is popular in states with a majority of the population but not in a majority of the states, it may pass in the House of Representatives, but fail in the Senate. Only if a law is both popular with a majority of the population as a whole and in a majority of states is it likely to pass both houses. After that, the president may veto the law (subject to the two-thirds congressional override) if he believes it is contrary to the public interest. Yet still, the courts may strike it down if they determine it is unconstitutional.

N. By requiring significant support across different constituencies in society, the Constitution makes passing laws very difficult. Some people complain about "gridlock" in Washington: the houses of Congress and the president cannot agree about what to do, and so little gets done. The Framers would likely have had little patience with this complaint. They intentionally wrote a constitution that requires the concurrence of many in order to ensure the tremendous power of government is used wisely in a way that a good majority of the people are likely to think wise— and that is the best guarantee that it really will be wise.

O. This system of pitting public official against public official and creating incentives so public officials will act in the public interest permeates the Constitution. *"In a single republic,"* Madison writes, *"all the power surrendered by the people is* *submitted to the administration of a single government; and the usurpations are guarded against by a division of the government into distinct and separate departments,"* - meaning the separation of powers in the legislative, executive, and judicial branches of government. In America however, power *"is first divided between two distinct governments,"* meaning the federal government and the states, *"and then the portion allotted to each [is] subdivided among distinct and separate departments* (No. 51)." The division of government power between the federal government and the state governments is known as the *vertical separation of powers*, and the division within each level of the legislative, executive, and judicial departments is known as the *horizontal separation of powers.* By using this dual separation, *"a double security arises to the rights of the people"* for the *"different governments will control each other, at the same time that each will be controlled by itself* (No. 51)."

P. In perhaps the most ingenious application of the principle, the Framers realized the larger the country, the better the principle will work. Public officials elected by different groups of people in different parts of a large country will inevitably represent the interests of those who elect them. *"What are the different classes of legislators but advocates and parties to the causes which they determine* (No. 10)?" In a large country like America, you *"extend the sphere, and you take in a greater variety of parties and interests,"* and in this way *"you make it less probable that a majority of the whole will have a common motive to invade the rights of other citizens* (No. 10)." In theory, for each special interest, there will be an opposed special interest, as well as a large population not likely to be biased one way or the other. This disinterested group can best judge which party's position corresponds with the public interest and throw its support behind that group.

Q. The Securities Exchange Act of 1934 is a good example of the special interest principle in action. Under the provisions of this act, corporate executives can be sued for securities fraud if they misrepresent the status of their corporation's business. The executives don't like this, and are constantly lobbying Congress to restrict such lawsuits. They argue many of the suits brought are frivolous; the lawyers who bring them do so only to collect a fee, and the suits provide no real benefit to the corporation's shareholders. The lawyers who bring the suits, of course, see things quite differently: They say the government lacks resources to detect cases of securities fraud. Without the lawyers' efforts, corporate managers committing fraud would never be caught, thus the integrity of the marketplace ultimately depends on their efforts, which entitle them to the fees they earn.

R. So, here we have two special interests—corporate executives and trial lawyers—each with a personal stake in the matter, and both lobbying Congress about how best to deter securities fraud without overburdening companies with frivolous lawsuits. One special interest tends to balance out the other, and, in recent years, Congress has made changes to the securities laws that have reduced the number of frivolous lawsuits without allowing real fraudsters to go unpunished. It is a messy system, but, as the Framers envisioned, it tends to produce tolerably good results.

S. One final thought about why this should be important to you. As Benjamin Franklin was leaving the last meeting of the Philadelphia Convention, someone asked him what kind of government the convention had designed. He answered, "A republic—if you can keep it." He meant that, no matter what the Framers wrote on paper, the system would endure only if the American people remained intelligent, informed, interested in questions of the public good, and ready to participate in the processes of government. As Hamilton put it:

[I]t seems to have been reserved to the people of this country, by their conduct and example, to decide the important question, whether societies of men are really capable or not of establishing good government from reflection and choice, or whether they are forever destined to depend for their political constitutions on accident and force. (No. 1)

That question has to be answered, again and again, by each generation of Americans. Over the course of your lifetime, the responsibility will be yours to ensure "government of the people, by the people, for the people, shall not perish from the earth."

8

If Men Were Angels, No Government Would Be Necessary

Political Freedom in the *Federalist Papers* by Stephen B. Presser

Federalist Papers referenced in essay: #10, 44, 51, 84

A. "Political Freedom," or as the authors of the *Federalist Papers* refer to it, "The Science of Politics," is what everything in the *Federalist Papers* is about. Hamilton, Madison, and Jay's purpose was to write about how the proposed constitution created a form of government that would make it possible for politics to work in America. The three were concerned that after the break with Great Britain in 1776, the governments of the thirteen states were not functioning properly. They were not protecting the basic rights of the citizens. For the authors of the *Federalist Papers,* the science of politics and politics itself were about how best to secure the rights of the people, and how to make sure that governments and people did not endanger those rights.   The challenge for the authors of the *Federalist Papers* was to show how the kind of republican government contemplated by the proposed constitution would be the best way to preserve basic rights. Their adoption of the name "Publius," after Publius Valerius Publicola, one of the Founders and saviors of republican Rome, was designed to suggest just that.

B. When Hamilton, Madison, and Jay invoked republican

Rome, they had a vision somewhat different from the politics practiced in this country today. For us, politics is about the government providing services, regulating activity, or redistributing wealth to secure social welfare. For the Framers of the Constitution, however, the science of politics and the practice of politics were all about how to distribute power within the government in order to preserve private property, individual rights, and the rule of law which secured both. The authors of the *Federalist Papers* are especially worried about the majority trampling the property and rights of the minority, as was then happening in individual states.

C. As Madison says,

To secure the public good and private rights against the danger of such a [majority] faction, and at the same time to preserve the spirit and the form of popular government, is then the great object to which our enquiries are directed. (No. 10)

The goal of the *Federalist Papers* was to explain how a republican (or representative) government based on the sovereignty of the people could still protect rights *and* proceed according to the rule of law.

D. We often speak of our government as a democracy (direct rule by the people), but the truth is we have always had a republic, not a democracy. In a pure democracy, a faction composed of a majority of the citizens would be likely to endanger the persons or property of particular individuals or groups, but a republic, "*by which I mean a Government in which the scheme of representation takes place, opens a different prospect, and promises the cure for which we are seeking* (No. 10)." Madison argues a representative form of government (a republic) is better than a democracy because it results in a system of government which will

refine and enlarge the public views, by passing them
through the medium of a chosen body of citizens, whose
wisdom may best discern the true interest of their country,
and whose patriotism and love of justice will be least likely
to sacrifice it to temporary or partial considerations. (No.
10)

E. Madison goes on to make one of the most brilliant and bold
assertions regarding republican government. Until the *Federalist
Papers*, it was generally believed that a republic (a government
composed of representatives of the people, rather than rule by
aristocrats or a monarch) could only function in a small territory,
and for a small group of people. Madison recognizes that
sometimes *"men of factious tempers, of local prejudices, or of
sinister designs, may, by intrigue, by corruption, or by other
means, first obtain [election], and then betray the interests, of the
people."* The threat of such betrayal could be reduced, however, if
the republic was large in territory and composed of many people.
In such a territory, noxious factions would cancel each other out,
and result in representatives *"whose enlightened views and
virtuous sentiments render them superior to local prejudices, and
to schemes of injustice."* Madison also suggests *"the increased
variety of parties,"* will *"consist in the greater obstacles opposed
to the concert and accomplishment of the secret wishes of an
unjust and [self-]interested majority* (No. 10)."

F. The arguments in the *Federalist Papers* are all about
controlling the government and avoiding an abusive government.
Still, the *Federalist Papers,* and the Constitution itself, are as much
about duty and responsibility as they are about the preservation of
individual rights. A well-balanced and ordered government is the
only guarantee of really important rights, such as those to security
of person and property. The Framers of the Constitution and the
writers of the *Federalist Papers* knew history revealed republics

often degenerated into what they called "factions," which are not terribly different from our own political parties.

G. Such factions have existed since before the Constitution was written. American politics is a constant struggle, with no long-term winners or gainers. However, it appears Americans have achieved a higher standard of living and a greater accumulation of wealth than the people of most other nations. We have managed this, in general, because the constitutional structure envisioned by the Framers has saved us from ourselves. The best illustrations of the perspective of the Framers are the famous statements made by Madison in No. 51. *"Ambition,"* said Madison, *"must be made to counteract ambition. The interest of the man must be connected with the constitutional rights of the place."* By this, Madison means human beings are rather selfish and self-interested creatures. It was necessary to recognize that fact and use these characteristics to reach something better. Madison continues, using perhaps the most famous words he ever wrote:

> *It may be a reflection on human nature, that such devices should be necessary to control the abuses of government. But what is government itself, but the greatest of all reflections on human nature? If men were angels, no government would be necessary. If angels were to govern men, neither external nor internal controls on government would be necessary. In framing a government which is to be administered by men over men, the great difficulty lies in this: you must first enable the government to control the governed; and in the next place oblige it to control itself. A dependence on the people, is no doubt, the primary control on the government; but experience has taught mankind the necessity of auxiliary precautions.*
> (No. 51)

H. The "internal" controls to which Madison refers are the checks and balances among each branch of the government—the legislative, the executive, and the judicial—keeping each other within the specified bounds of the Constitution. The "external" controls would be applied by the states, which would ensure the federal government went no further than the Constitution permits. *"Hence a double security arises to the rights of the people. The different governments will control each other, at the same time that each will be controlled by itself* (No. 51)." In our era, when the federal government is involved in many areas that were formerly the exclusive responsibilities of the state and local governments, the reflections in No. 51 are particularly relevant.

I. The *Federalist Papers* are particularly brilliant in explaining a constitutional structure designed to save us from ourselves. The authors recognize a discernible purpose to politics; the shimmering constitutional structure exists for a compelling reason. In his preface of the collected first volume of the *Federalist Papers* from 1788, Hamilton says, "The great wish is that [the *Federalist Papers]* may promote the cause of truth and lead to a right judgment of the true interests of the community," which Hamilton believes would be furthered by ratifying the Constitution. But what is this "truth"? What are "the true interests of the community"?

J. For the authors of the *Federalist Papers* there are things a government is supposed to do, and indeed, it all boils down to this: *"Justice is the end of government. It is the end of civil society. It ever has been and ever will be pursued, until it be obtained, or until liberty be lost in the pursuit* (No. 51)." We talk a lot about liberty in this country, but it is important to understand for the Framers, the pursuit of justice is even more important than individual liberty. How, then, was the new government to pursue justice? On one aspect of the pursuit, the *Federalist Papers* is stunningly clear. There are some things that are clearly the job of a good government to resist. These limitations on government are very nicely laid out in No. 10.

K. Madison recognizes an age-old problem in governance: what to do about the inevitably unequal distribution of wealth in society. Madison understands individuals have different qualities and abilities, and that from these *"unequal faculties of men"* comes the unequal distribution of property. Madison says it is from these unequal faculties *"from which the rights of property originate"* and it is *"the first object of government"* to protect those faculties. Madison recognizes these unequal faculties and the resultant difference in the distribution of property will lead to trouble. He states:

> *the most common and durable source of factions has been the various and unequal distribution of property. Those who hold and those who are without property have ever formed distinct interests in society. Those who are creditors, and those who are debtors, fall under a like discrimination. A landed interest, a manufacturing interest, a mercantile interest, a moneyed interest, with many lesser interests, grow up of necessity in civilized nations, and divide them into different classes, actuated by different sentiments and views. The regulation of these various and interfering interests forms the principal task of modern legislation, and involves the spirit of party and faction in the necessary and ordinary operations of government.* (No. 10)

The difficult task for the new government was to secure property through the regulation of the "various and interfering interests" in society, and if possible, reign in "the spirit of party and faction."

L. Thus, Madison warns against *"a rage for paper money, for* *an abolition of debts, for an equal division of property, or for any other improper or wicked project* (No. 10)." Issuing worthless paper money and abolishing debts were all actions tempting the state governments. For Madison, these activities were "improper or wicked." These are the very things a government must not do. The federal government should not take these actions and should seek to prevent state governments from doing them, too. Such prohibitions, Madison notes, will *"banish speculations on public measures, inspire a general prudence and industry, and give a regular course to the business of society* (No. 44)."

M. Another feature of the political theory of the Constitution's Framers and the authors of the *Federalist Papers* is that it was important to restrain the exercise of power by government officials. This could be handled several ways: creating a system of checks and balances among the legislative, executive, and judicial branches to minimize the impact of untrustworthy persons; giving power to both state and federal governments to further divide the various centers of power in the nation; and finally, designing a system of regular and frequent elections to increase turnover among those in power, preventing consolidation and corruption. The Founders at the Constitutional Convention knew that since independence, demagogues seeking power for its own sake or to use in corrupt financial schemes carried a disproportionate influence in the state governments. It was his fear that such men might lead factions in the states or in the federal government. This led to Madison's clear condemnation of faction and his theory that factions could best be controlled in a large territory.

N. Parallels exist between our modern national and cultural commitment to diversity and Madison's vision of what was necessary for the eighteenth century American republic. Likening the manner in which religious freedom is preserved by tolerance for many religions, he states:

in a free government the security for civil rights must be
the same as for religious rights. It consists in the one case
in the multiplicity of interests, and in the other in the
multiplicity of sects. The degree of security in both cases
will depend on the number of interests and sects; and this
may be presumed to depend on the extent of country and
number of people comprehended under the same
government. (No. 51)

Elaborating on this theme, and brilliantly and historically creating a new argument that the best guarantee of proper functioning in a republic is to have a large one, he wrote:

in the extended republic of the United States, and among
the great variety of interests, parties, and sects which it
embraces, a coalition of a majority of the whole society
could seldom take place on any other principles than
those of justice and the general good; whilst there being
thus less danger to a minor from the will of the major
party, there must be less pretext, also, to provide for the
security of the former, by introducing into the government
a will not dependent on the latter, or, in other words, a
will independent of the society itself. (No. 51)

O. Madison believed there are clearly discernible principles of "justice and the general good," and for the government to function according to those principles, factions must be controlled. The majority must not be permitted to trample the rights of the minority. The experience of mankind had shown *"measures are too often decided, not according to the rules of justice and the rights of the minor party, but by the superior force of an interested and over bearing majority* (No. 10)." Thus, the structural protections in the new constitution were designed to prevent the malevolent operations of *"an interested and over bearing* *majority*." Madison argues that by creating a larger electorate, Americans would create a situation where more "fit characters" would be able to run for office, and it would be more difficult for *"unworthy candidates to practice with success the vicious arts by which elections are too often carried."* Ultimately, however, Madison puts his trust in the wisdom and virtue of the American people themselves, when he expresses his hope that *"the suffrages of the people being more free, [they] will be more likely to centre in men who possess the most attractive merit and the most diffusive and established characters* (No. 10)."

P. The ideas then, of a large republic; of dual state and federal sovereignty; of separation of powers and checks and balances; in short, of the entire structure of the Constitution itself, are the guarantees of the political rights of the American people. Critics of the Constitution however, were skeptical. They believed the Constitution was deeply flawed because in its original form it contained no bill of rights. There were no express guarantees of popular freedoms such as freedom of the press, freedom of speech, freedom of religion, freedom of assembly, or freedom from unreasonable searches and seizures. It is those popular freedoms that we usually think as constituting political freedom, but this was not the vision of the *Federalist Papers* authors. It is important to understand why some proponents of the Constitution, including Hamilton, thought the absence of such a bill of rights was one of the strengths and not one of the weaknesses of the proposed national government. Hamilton addresses this issue in No. 84.

Q. For Hamilton, the genius of the proposed federal constitution is it creates a federal government of limited and enumerated rights. There are some things the federal government could do, for example, the regulation of commerce and the ability to wage war and protect national security, but for most tasks of government, the federal government was to leave things to the states or the people therein. A federal government limited in its scope is one more security for the rights of the people. Thus, for Hamilton, adding a bill of rights to the Constitution would be *"not only unnecessary,"* but *"would even be dangerous."* This is because such a bill of rights

> *would contain various exceptions to powers not granted; and, on this very account, would afford a colorable pretext to claim more than were granted. For why declare that things shall not be done which there is no power to do? Why, for instance, should it be said that the liberty of the press shall not be restrained, when no power is given by which restrictions may be imposed? I will not contend that such a provision would confer a regulating power; but it is evident that it would furnish, to men disposed to usurp, a plausible pretense for claiming that power. They might urge with a semblance of reason, that the Constitution ought not to be charged with the absurdity of providing against the abuse of an authority which was not given, and that the provision against restraining the liberty of the press afforded a clear implication, that a power to prescribe proper regulations concerning it was intended to be vested in the national government. This may serve as a specimen of the numerous handles which would be given to the doctrine of constructive powers, by the indulgence of an injudicious zeal for bills of rights.*
> (No. 84)

In a limited government, there is no need to specify the rights reserved to the states or people, because all such rights and all powers, other than those *expressly* granted by the Constitution, belong and will always belong to the people and their state and local governments. What the federal Constitution and what the *Federalist Papers* were designed to do, was to preserve for the

American people the most important political right of all: self-government.

R. Those who have understood that point have lavished praise on the *Federalist Papers* in superlatives that are almost embarrassing, except for the fact that they are correct. Thomas Jefferson describes the *Federalist Papers* as "the best commentary on the principles of government, which ever was written." Clinton Rossiter, in his 1961 introduction to the *Federalist Papers,* describes it as "the most important work in political science that has ever been written, or is likely ever to be written in the United States. It is, indeed, the one product of the American mind that is rightly counted among the classics of political theory." Jacob Cooke, another editor of the *Federalist Papers,* says the *Federalist* is "the most significant contribution Americans have made to political philosophy." In our era, as in the late eighteenth century, there is a great risk that our government will increase in power and the rights of property and self-government will be increasingly threatened. We can still learn much about political freedom from the Framers, and from Hamilton, Madison, and Jay.

9

Money is, With Propriety, Considered as the Vital Principle of the Body Politic

The *Federalist Papers* and Economic Freedom

by Evan M. Koster

Federalist Papers referenced in essay: #1, 2, 5, 7, 8, 10, 12, 30, 41, 42, 44, 54, 85

A. The *Federalist Papers* are organized under two broad themes, "Union" and "The Merits of the Constitution." Neither of these themes obviously has anything to do with economic freedom, and a quick review of the titles of the various essays does not reveal a particular interest in economic issues. From No. 2 ("Concerning Dangers from Foreign Force and Influence"), No. 21 ("Other defects of the Present Confederation"), and No. 51 ("The Structure of the Government Must Furnish the Proper Checks and Balances Between the Different Departments), it appears the *Federalist Papers* are entirely concerned with political theory, relations between the states, and relations among the states and foreign governments. In fact, the term "economic freedom" is never used in the essays.

B. A deeper dive into the essays, however, reveals the *Federalist Papers* are not agnostic on the topic of economic freedom. The essays are a useful guide and provide an explanation as to how the Constitution and the structure of government reflected in the Constitution can serve to enhance economic freedoms and liberty. This does not mean economic factors and interests *alone* explain the structure of government reflected in the Constitution. While such interests may provide some background and explain motivations of the Framers, these preferences alone cannot explain the complete structure of republican government ultimately adopted, or its utility today in preserving economic freedom and choice. The *Federalist Papers* do not see the Constitution as setting up a political structure which can be used to favor one social class or "faction" over another. Instead, the *Papers* enable us to understand how the form of republican government embedded in the Constitution ensures all groups have the equality of opportunity to pursue their economic interests and economic freedoms free from the distractions of international and domestic conflict, free from the oppression of an interested majority, and free from the excessive influence of a divisive faction.

C. The economic problems experienced under the Articles of Confederation are well documented. At the time, the federal government held little power to raise revenue and repay its debt. In order to pay for revolutionary wartime expenses, Congress borrowed money from European countries, and when this was not enough, Congress printed more money, leading to inflation. Ultimately, Congress resorted to a voluntary system of requisition where each state was to collect a proportionate share of the federal budget from the inhabitants of its state. As a strictly voluntary system without enforcement powers, Congress found it difficult to even pay for a standing army.

D. The limitations inherent in the Articles of Confederation stem from the fear of creating a strong central government like that of Britain. As a result, significant power was retained by state governments. Congress had little or no authority to enforce laws, tax, regulate trade, or ensure the uniform application of federal standards to the states. A single state could block an attempt to enhance any powers of Congress.

E. In this setting, individual states sought to enhance the economic interests of themselves and their residents. Many states began to violate the treaties arranged between the U.S. and European countries. These states began levying taxes on foreign goods--even though Congress was granted the sole authority to control trade between states and foreign countries. Individual states began to impose import levies on goods from other states. States that shared the same rivers even imposed competing tolls.

F. Territorial disputes between states were common. States with well-defined boundaries, such as the Atlantic Ocean, argued that unsettled territories to the west belonged to all states and should be administered by the federal government. States whose original charters granted them land west of the Appalachian Mountains argued the western land was theirs. Sometimes these territorial disputes led to violence.

G. Tensions boiled over in western Massachusetts in January 1787, when indebted small farmers organized under Daniel Shays and seized a federal arsenal of weapons to protest increased taxes and debt foreclosures. The resulting violence helped to convince doubters that a strong central government was necessary.

H. In that environment, three major obstacles stood in the way of economic freedom. With no uniform system of rules governing economic conduct, individual efforts to improve their own economic situation had little chance of succeeding. There was no neutral institution that would enforce uniform rules. Merchants and other economic interests faced at least thirteen different sets of laws and regulations. Finally, without a strong central republican government and with thirteen states intent on promoting their own interests, free and open competition was not achievable.

I. The treatment of economic freedom within the *Federalist Papers* corresponds to the division of the essays into two parts. The first group of essays makes the case that the present structure under the Articles of Confederation was not working, and only a stronger union can resolve the issues. The second set of essays makes the case for the Constitution against the charges leveled by the critics. In fact, Hamilton promises a discussion of *"the additional security which its adoption will afford to the preservation of that species of government, to liberty, and to property* (No. 1)."

J. Quoting a letter by a British monarch, John Jay emphasizes a union *"must increase your strength, riches, and trade; and by this union the whole island, being joined in affection and free from all apprehensions of different interest, will be ENABLED TO RESIST ALL ITS ENEMIES* (No. 5)." Jay uses Britain's history as an example of a nation that prospered once divisions and jealousies were extinguished.

> *Should the people of America divide into three or four nations, would not the same thing happen? Would not similar jealousies arise, and be in like manner cherished? Instead of their being 'joined in affection' and free from all apprehensions of different 'interests,' envy and jealousy would soon extinguish confidence and affection, and the partial interests of each confederacy, instead of the general interests of all America, would be the only objects of their policy and pursuits.* (No. 5)

K. Hamilton carries this line of argument further when he explains how competition and discrimination among states can frustrate the expansion of commerce and the spirit of enterprise in commercial America.

*The competitions of commerce would be another fruitful
source of contention. The States less favorably
circumstanced would be desirous of escaping from the
disadvantages of local situation, and of sharing in the
advantages of their more fortunate neighbors. Each
State, or separate confederacy, would pursue a system of
commercial policy peculiar to itself. This would occasion
distinctions, preferences, and exclusions, which would
beget discontent. The habits of intercourse, on the basis
of equal privileges, to which we have been accustomed
since the earliest settlement of the country, would give a
keener edge to those causes of discontent than they would
naturally have independent of this circumstance. WE
SHOULD BE READY TO DENOMINATE INJURIES
THOSE THINGS WHICH WERE IN REALITY THE
JUSTIFIABLE ACTS OF INDEPENDENT
SOVEREIGNTIES CONSULTING A DISTINCT
INTEREST. The spirit of enterprise, which characterizes
the commercial part of America, has left no occasion of
displaying itself unimproved. It is not at all probable that
this unbridled spirit would pay much respect to those
regulations of trade by which particular States might
endeavor to secure exclusive benefits to their own
citizens. The infractions of these regulations, on one side,
the efforts to prevent and repel them, on the other, would
naturally lead to outrages, and these to reprisals and
wars.* (No. 7)

L. Hamilton also provides examples of how the authority of
each state to impose taxes upon the residents of other states will
lead to impediments for growth in markets. In addition, *"laws in
violation of private contracts, as they amount to aggressions on the
rights of those States whose citizens are injured by them"* will
result from the disunity of the states and lack of a strong central

government. These laws could hardly be conducive to an environment of free and open competition.

M. According to Hamilton, the ultimate result will be war between the states. This will further erode liberty because

> *[e]ven the ardent love of liberty will, after a time, give way to its dictates. The violent destruction of life and property incident to war, the continual effort and alarm attendant on a state of continual danger, will compel nations the most attached to liberty to resort for repose and security to institutions which have a tendency to destroy their civil and political rights. To be more safe, they at length become willing to run the risk of being less free.* (No. 8)

N. James Madison, another author of the *Federalist Papers,* focuses his attention to the danger of factions. He outlines how the lack of a strong central government creates an environment in which factions can proliferate and economic liberty can be limited. According to Madison, the unequal distribution of property will cause a faction that allows men to oppress each other, rather than work towards the common good.

> *Those who hold and those who are without property have ever formed distinct interests in society. Those who are creditors, and those who are debtors, fall under a like discrimination. A landed interest, a manufacturing interest, a mercantile interest, a moneyed interest, with many lesser interests, grow up of necessity in civilized nations, and divide them into different classes, actuated by different sentiments and views. The regulation of these various and interfering interests forms the principal task of modern legislation, and involves the spirit of party and faction in the necessity and ordinary operations of the*

government. (No. 10)

O. In asserting the dangers from unequal distribution of property, Madison is not advocating policies that "redistributed" or "spread the wealth." Rather, Madison is revealing the dangers of a political system which does not have a level playing field in terms of factions having equal opportunity to advocate their cause. In such a system, the most numerous party or the most powerful faction will prevail at the expense of "justice." Relief from this inequality of opportunity is not achieved by removing the causes of faction (i.e. the unequal distribution of property), but by controlling its effect through republican government. A republican form of government can act as the neutral referee among these factions so the conditions for economic opportunity and open competition can exist.

P. The remedy—republican government—will also allow individuals to yield results based upon their own efforts and abilities.

> *By multiplying the means of gratification, by promoting the introduction and circulation of the precious metals, those darling objects of human avarice and enterprise, it serves to vivify and invigorate the channels of industry, and to make them flow with greater activity and copiousness. The assiduous merchant, the laborious husbandman, the active mechanic, and the industrious manufacturer, —all order of men, look forward with eager expectation and growing alacrity to this pleasing reward of their toils.* (No. 12)

Q. This government must be given the tools in order to enforce its powers and facilitate the expansion of commerce. One such tool is the authority to tax and procure a national currency.

Money is, with propriety, considered as the vital principle
of the body politic; as that which sustains its life and
motion, and enables it to perform its most essential
functions. A complete power, therefore, to procure a
regular and adequate supply of it, as far as the resources
of the community will permit, may be regarded as an
indispensable ingredient in every constitution. From a
deficiency in this particular, one of two evils must ensue;
either the people must be subjected to continual plunder,
as a substitute for a more eligible mode of supplying the
public wants, or the government must sink into a fatal
atrophy, and, in a short course of time, perish. (No. 30)

R. Madison's views on the powers conferred by the
Constitution are that they had, among their objectives, several
goals which relate directly to economic freedom, namely:
"Regulation of the intercourse with foreign nations. . . .
Maintenance of harmony and proper intercourse among the States.
. . . Restraint of the States from certain injurious acts (No. 41)." To
ensure the latter, the Constitution, through the Commerce Clause,
vests in the federal government the right to control commerce
between the states. Madison argues this power, by prohibiting
discriminatory acts by one state against the residents of another
state, will facilitate commerce. The Constitution, by authorizing
Congress to pass uniform laws, will prevent inconsistent state laws
which could act as barriers to free and open competition.

S. Extolling the virtues of the Constitution in giving the federal
government power to establish bankruptcy laws, Madison explains:

The power of establishing uniform laws of bankruptcy is
so intimately connected with the regulation of commerce,
and will prevent so many frauds where the parties or their
property may lie or be removed into different States, that

the expediency of it seems not likely to be drawn into question. (No. 42)

T. Other restrictions on the authority of the several states that will promote trade include the right of coining money and issuing currency. As Madison states:

> *Had every State a right to regulate the value of its coin, there might be as many different currencies as States, and thus the intercourse among them would be impeded; retrospective alterations in its value might be made, and thus the citizens of other States be injured, and animosities be kindled among the States themselves.* (No. 44)

U. It is not only the supremacy of the federal government that will enable economic freedom to flourish, according to the authors of the *Federalist Papers,* but also the system of checks and balances between the various branches of the federal government embedded in the Constitution. While the Constitution must enable the federal government to control the nation, the government must be able to control itself. Due to the various checks and balances on each branch of government, the rights of individuals—including economic rights—will not be in danger from "interested combinations of the majority."

V. Nowhere is this self-check on the ability of the federal government to restrain liberty more evident than in the structure of the House of Representatives. First, according to No. 52, the qualifications for the representatives are based strictly on merit, without regard to poverty or wealth or to any particular profession of religious faith. Second, the frequency of the elections, every two years, ensures the House will be more responsive to the electorate than to the other more permanent branches of government. Third, proportionate representation, as set forth in the

Constitution for the House, reflects a merit based system in which, according to No. 54, *"[a]s far, therefore, as their superior wealth and weight may justly entitle them to any advantage, it ought to be secured to them by a superior share of representation."* Citizens who might have concerns about encroachments upon their economic liberties will have ample opportunities to make their concerns known each election day.

W. Further, by providing for a second chamber, the Senate, whose members are designated by a different process for different terms but with equal representation, the Constitution has embedded another check on the ability of the legislature to restrict economic freedom. As set forth in No. 62, the Senate

> *as a second branch of the legislative assembly, distinct from, and dividing the power with, a first, must be in all cases a salutary check on the government. It doubles the security to the people, by requiring the concurrence of two distinct bodies in schemes of usurpation or perfidy, where the ambition or corruption of one would otherwise be sufficient.*

This structure makes it exceedingly difficult to curb the American entrepreneurial spirit.

X. The judiciary also has a significant role in preserving economic liberty. According to Hamilton in No. 78:

> *This independence of the judges is equally requisite to guard the Constitution and the rights of individuals from the effects of those ill humors, which the arts of designing men, or the influence of particular conjunctures, sometimes disseminate among the people themselves, and which, though they speedily give place to better information, and more deliberate reflection, have a*

tendency, in the meantime, to occasion dangerous
innovations in the government, and serious oppressions of
the minor party in the community.

This independent judiciary serves as a final check on the unbridled concentration of federal power.

Y. The *Federalist Papers* reveal it is not the intent of the Constitution to prefer one economic group over another, or one economic outcome versus another. By enhancing the authority of the federal government, empowering it with the authority to tax, coin money, and regulate interstate commerce, the federal government is given the tools to act as the impartial arbiter or referee in disputes among the states. Lest it become too powerful and a vehicle for powerful factions to dominate the weak, numerous checks and balances are embedded in the Constitution through a dual chamber legislature. Each chamber has specific enumerated requirements designed to maximize its effectiveness while avoiding the concentration of power and the limitation of liberties. The *Federalist Papers* reveal the objective of the Constitution is not to enshrine economic equality, but create the political structure and opportunities so economic freedom and economic liberty can prevail. As Hamilton so eloquently noted:

The additional securities to republican government, to
liberty and to property, to be derived from the adoption of
the plan under consideration, consist chiefly in the
restraints which the preservation of the Union will impose
on local factions and insurrections, and on the ambition
of powerful individuals in single States, who may acquire
credit and influence enough, from leaders and favorites,
to become the despots of the people; in the diminution of
the opportunities to foreign intrigue, which the dissolution
of the Confederacy would invite and facilitate; in the

prevention of extensive military establishments, which
could not fail to grow out of wars between the States in a
disunited situation; in the express guaranty of a
republican form of government to each; in the absolute
and universal exclusion of titles of nobility; and in the
precautions against the repetition of those practices on
the part of the State governments which have undermined
the foundations of property and credit, have planted
mutual distrust in the breasts of all classes of citizens, and
have occasioned an almost universal prostration of
morals. (No. 85)

10

The Security for Civil Rights Must Be the Same as That for Religious Rights

Religious Freedom in the *Federalist Papers*
by Matthew J. Franck

Federalist Papers referenced in essay: #1, 2, 10, 23, 48, 51, 52, 55, 84

Editors' Note: For a wide variety of reasons (as discussed in the following essay), religious freedom is not treated in any significant detail in the Federalist Papers. *However, for other reasons (also discussed in the essay), religious liberty was very much on the minds of the Founders. No book that attempts to "unlock" the* Roots of Liberty *would be complete without a treatment of the Founders' understanding of freedom of religion, and it is within such a spirit of inquiry that this essay is included.*

A. Questions of religion, religious freedom, and religious strife are not major themes of the *Federalist Papers*. Not one of Publius' eighty-five essays takes the protection of religious liberty as a distinct subject worthy of a sustained focus. Yet, we know during this period of American history, from the revolution through the ratification and amendment of the Constitution (1775-1791), the protection of religious liberty, and the proper relationship of religion to politics, were of great concern to the Founders. Why, then, in the single most important contemporaneous commentary on the Constitution, do the authors have so little to say on this subject? And when the subject is treated—always just in passing—what do the *Federalist Papers* have to teach us about religious freedom?

B. In the midst of the Revolutionary War, after the Continental Congress passed the Declaration of Independence in 1776, most of the thirteen former colonies—now calling themselves states—created constitutions for themselves. These replaced royal charters that were now either of no use, or fundamentally flawed as charters for self-governing republics. Most of these new state constitutions had something to say on the subject of religion and religious freedom, since most American states exhibited a good deal of religious diversity, and many had been settled by refugees from religious persecution. Practically all Americans were Christians, though there were a few Jews. Practically all Christians were Protestants, though there was a substantial Catholic population in Maryland.

C. However, the diversity among the Protestants was considerable: Episcopalian, Presbyterian, Congregationalist, Dutch Reformed, Methodist, Baptist, and Quaker. In the politics of the newly independent states, it was vital these groups accommodate one another peaceably, and not make their different beliefs the basis of political conflict. Everyone should be free to worship as he or she saw fit, without being coerced to believe (or pretend to believe) in the doctrines of an official faith. On this much, all agreed.

D. But, much else was negotiable. Should office holding be restricted to Christians, or even more narrowly to Protestants? (Most of the states had some test of this sort.) Could a state recognize one particular church as privileged over others, even while leaving people otherwise free to worship where and as they please? Should tax dollars support religious ministries or religious education? If so, should citizens be entitled to direct their own tax dollars to support ministries of their choosing—or to opt out altogether? To these questions, states gave widely different answers.

E. In the state of Virginia, a certain religious controversy is much remembered today because James Madison was in the thick of it. The state's new constitution, adopted in 1776, had a strong statement on religious freedom. As a result, the Episcopal Church, which had served as the established (official) church of the Virginia colony, largely lost its predominant position. But in 1785, a bill was proposed in the Virginia legislature to support Christian clergymen with tax dollars. Madison successfully opposes it in a petition famously known as the *Memorial and Remonstrance.* He argues that such legislation interferes with the rights of individual conscience and the duties men owe first to the "Governor of the Universe" before any human government. The clergy-supported bill was defeated. But, the very next year the Virginia legislature adopted Thomas Jefferson's *Virginia Statute for Religious Freedom.* This law bolstered the protection already in the state constitution. From this episode, we know Madison was deeply concerned about state limitations on all freedoms, especially religious freedom. The lack of much discussion of this subject in the *Federalist Papers* cannot be taken as evidence that the authors did not care, but, rather, they had little or no concern about the federal government's potential for limiting religious liberty.

F. America's first attempt at a constitution binding states together, the Articles of Confederation, did not contain any provision on religious freedom. But the presumption of the Articles is nearly all the important business of politics is to take place at the level of the states, with the Confederation loosely uniting them for defense and diplomacy. When the Constitution was drafted in 1787, its aim was to change that equation and give a new national government much more responsibility for the internal affairs of the United States. Still, the states would presumably remain closest to the people's everyday lives (an idea the *Federalist Papers* themselves underscore repeatedly). Many of the specific protections of individual liberty—including religious liberty—that one commonly found in the state constitutions were not thought to be necessary or appropriate in the new constitution. The Framers believe issues related to religious freedom would mostly occur in the context of state laws and policies, and be governed by each state's constitution.

G. Moreover, the *Federalist Papers* is a series of essays intended to defend the proposed constitution and advance the cause of its ratification by the states. The three authors have no interest in picking unnecessary fights by pointing to things the Framers left *out* of the Constitution. They are concerned with defending what is *in* the Constitution, and the way in which it fundamentally reforms—for the better—the relationship of the states to the nation, and the relationship of the people to both levels of government.

H. The Constitution does make one statement about religious liberty. Article VI, Section 3 requires public officials of the state and federal governments to take an oath to "support this Constitution," and then adds "but no religious Test shall ever be required as a Qualification to any Office or public Trust under the United States." The phrase was introduced by Charles Pinckney of South Carolina and elicited little debate or discussion during the Constitutional Convention. Even today this seems one of the least controversial clauses the Constitution could possibly contain. Madison never offers explanation or defense of it, merely alluding to it in No. 52 when he remarks service in the House of Representatives is *"open to merit of every description, whether native or adoptive, whether young or old, and without regard to poverty or wealth, or to any particular profession of religious faith."*

I. There are two major reasons that Article VI, Section 3 is barely referenced in the *Federalist Papers*. First, the most extended objections to the lack of a religious test were not raised until July 1788—and the last of the *Federalist Papers* was published in May 1788. (However, in January, some delegates to the Massachusetts Convention had noted the lack of a religious test for office contradicted the motivations of the earliest settlers, many of whom came to America to preserve their religious traditions.) Second, the authors did not anticipate there would be any significant opposition to these provisions. When Charles Pinckney presented this idea at the Convention, it was accepted almost without debate. The Framers did not expect any real concerns to be raised in the state ratifying conventions.

J. Yet, various Anti-Federalists objected to the clause. Why? Some openly worried that the "no religious Test" principle would permit non-Christians to hold public office. Others were concerned that "papists" (Catholics) or Jews could hold office. Still others thought the clause might open office holding to persons who believed in no God at all. A test for specifically Christian belief would be problematic, due to a wide variety of forms of Christianity. If one were not prepared to state up front what forms of religious belief were ruled *in,* it would be very difficult to state what was ruled *out.* And no one, it seems, was prepared to write "no Jews, Muslims, or atheists" into the text of the Constitution.

K. The July 1788 debates from the North Carolina ratifying conventions provide useful insights into concerns about "no religious test." Delegate Henry Abbot feared this would lead to "papists, deists, and Mahometans" taking office. David Caldwell wanted a test because "the Christian religion was best calculated, of all religions, to make good members of society on account of its morality."

L. Supporters of the clause argued that a religious test was, in and of itself, a limitation on religious liberty and contrary to American ideals. Supporter James Iredell commented, "I consider the clause under consideration as one of the strongest proofs . . . that it was the intention of those who formed this system to establish a general religious liberty in America." Samuel Spencer noted, "Religious tests have been the foundation of persecutions in all countries." Some delegates expressed concerns that requiring such a test would lead to an established church at the national level.

M. In general, Anti-Federalists throughout the country had three major reservations on the status of religion under the proposed constitution. 1) The "no religious Test" clause might result in the election of the "wrong" kind of people (and the definition of *wrong* varied from state to state); 2) The new federal government might interfere with the states' systems of preference for Christianity, Protestantism, or particular denominations, and several states' established churches could be threatened; and 3) Religious liberty in general would not be protected from invasion by the federal government. Some people held all three views at once.

N. It may seem as if the third reservation cannot be squared with the first two. However, it was common, at the time of the Founding, for political thinkers to be concerned about striking a balance between support for religion (owing to its perceived connection to sound morality) and freedom of religious belief. They did not automatically think that absolute equal status for all religious views was required by the principle of religious freedom, nor that complete religious equality was the best way to provide support for religion and thus for morality. Today, we are more inclined to think both, and thus insist on all religious views (and even irreligious views like agnosticism, atheism, or secularism) being treated equally. Many of the Framers would not agree.

O. However, the demand for a bill of rights turned out to be one of the most significant Anti-Federalist critiques. Nearly everyone agreed the federal government should be stronger than it had been under the ineffective Articles of Confederation, and it was not difficult to make the case that the Constitution filled the bill nicely. But the Framers' omission of a bill of rights—an idea considered and rejected in the Constitutional Convention—gave the Constitution's opponents their most powerful weapon. This omission was not enough to defeat the Constitution in any state. It was not even enough to force the amendment of the Constitution as a precondition of its ratification. But it was enough to produce, in about half the states' ratifying conventions, resolutions calling on the new Congress to propose amendments for the states to consider.

P. In the first session of the First Congress in the summer of 1789, James Madison, now a member of the new House of Representatives and eager to ensure ratification of the constitution, consolidated over thirty-seven proposed amendments and persisted in his campaign until a dozen proposed amendments were sent to the states. Ten of them were ratified by December 1791 and are popularly known as the *Bill of Rights*. The one that became the First Amendment begins with a protection of religious liberty: "Congress shall make no law respecting an establishment of religion, or prohibiting the free exercise thereof." This language satisfied those who wanted a general protection of religious freedom; those who wanted to prevent the establishment of an "official" or preferred church by the federal government; and those who wanted to prevent that government's interference with any preferences then existing at the state level.

Q. Given Madison's experience in 1785 with the Virginia controversy over support of clergymen, it is not surprising he also proposed an amendment that would protect the "rights of conscience" (as well as free speech and press, and jury trials) from violation *by the states*. While this proposed amendment survived the debate in the House, it was rejected by the Senate and not sent to the states. Madison later said this was the "most valuable" amendment of all, and he regretted its defeat.

R. Madison regarded a limit on states' authority over religious liberty as "more valuable" than the protection of religious liberty from federal power. He shared Alexander Hamilton's arguments (No. 84) for the omission of a bill of rights from the original Constitution. Statements of the rights the federal government was forbidden to violate, Hamilton argued, might be *"fine declarations,"* but no language we might place in the Constitution could be so precisely drafted as to secure those rights with perfect success, protecting everything that should be protected and no more than that. The language would require interpretation; interpretation would necessarily involve the branches of the very government one was trying to restrain; and the one restraint to which the government would answer would be the people's authority. Therefore, concrete freedoms, ultimately, *"must altogether depend on public opinion."* Madison and Hamilton were arguing a bill of rights added nothing to the Constitution. As Hamilton concludes (No. 84), the Constitution as it came from Philadelphia in its original form was *"itself in every rational sense, and to every useful purpose, A BILL OF RIGHTS,"* and would thus safeguard all liberties, including religious freedom. What did he mean?

S. The *Federalist Papers* emphasize the essential goal in designing a constitution for a free people is not the use of fine words about rights that amount only to "parchment barriers" against tyranny (No. 48), but, instead, the design of an "internal structure" (No. 23) that tilts all the outcomes of the political process in favor of freedom. Whether it was religious liberty, or freedom of speech and press, or the free use of one's ability to acquire property, the real protection was provided by federalism, the separation of powers and checks and balances, and other features of the Constitution's system of republican government. These principles themselves relied on public opinion, kept it at arm's length, and shaped and directed it in ways friendly to freedom.

T. From the very first essay, the *Federalist Papers* is skeptical that we can simply trust majority rule to maintain liberty. Even when people's motives are good, they can be misled into thinking they have all the answers, and justifiably force others to agree with them. Hamilton reminds his readers of bloody religious strife, still fresh in the memory of people only removed by a generation or two from European soil:

> *Nothing could be more ill-judged than that intolerant spirit which has, at all times, characterized political parties. For in politics, as in religion, it is equally absurd to aim at making proselytes by fire and sword. Heresies in either can rarely be cured by persecution.* (No. 1)

U. Over and over, the authors of the *Federalist Papers* pushed their readers to recognize the unique pitfall of a democratic republic: the principle of democratic rule can lead to the oppression of minorities, with the majority itself turning out to be freedom's enemy. Therefore, the most important goal of the Constitution is to restrain, channel, and moderate the great power of the majority, without abandoning the principle ideal in a republic that the people will ultimately rule.

V. This recurring theme is most comprehensively fleshed out when Madison (No. 10 and No. 51) makes the novel argument that majority rule at the level of the whole United States will be more trustworthy than majority rule at the level of any individual state. In the larger, more diverse political environment of the entire country, there will be many more "factions": self-forming groups of people, organizing and pressing their views in the public sphere. None of them will hold the upper hand as the majority and all will have to learn to make compromises with one another, accommodating each other's particular interests in order to form the shifting, temporary, cobbled-together majorities that can win elections and pass laws. In such an environment, there are no permanent winners and losers. Everyone wins some fights and loses others.

W. Madison explicitly includes different religious viewpoints in this political analysis. In addition to factions organized around economic self-interest, he considers *"zeal for different opinions concerning religion"* (No. 10) as a strong basis for organizing. But, in this new democratic republic, the urge to impose one's own view on the whole world, *"by fire and sword"* (No. 1) will be replaced by moderation, and toleration of fellow citizens' different views, precisely because *so many* different views exist, and power must be shared. *"In a free government the security for civil rights must be the same as that for religious rights. It consists in the one case in the multiplicity of interests, and in the other, in the multiplicity of sects* (No. 51)." He continues later in the same essay:

> *In the extended republic of the United States, and among the great variety of interests, parties, and sects which it embraces, a coalition of a majority of the whole society could seldom take place on any other principles than those of justice and the general good.*

X. This could be contrasted with a less favorable outlook in the smaller environment of a single state: *"A religious sect may degenerate into a political faction in a part of the Confederacy; but the variety of sects dispersed over the entire face of it must secure the national councils against any danger from that source* (No. 10)." This helps explain why Madison, in the First Congress, thought a constitutional statement protecting religious liberty (and other freedoms) from *state* governments was more vital than a similar statement aimed at the new federal government. The states could be restrained by the federal government, but for restraining the federal government itself, a different calculation was required, as no political authority higher than itself would exist. In national politics, a free and dynamic process of democratic rule would be its own best insurance policy, supplemented by the backup mechanisms of the separation of powers, and checks and balances among the branches of government.

Y. If Madison seems skeptical of the good motives of religious citizens, does that mean he is skeptical of religion? Or does he think of religious faith as sometimes inclining people toward bad behavior rather than good? Not at all. He is realistic about what Christians call man's "fallen" nature, and is concerned with giving our politics a structure and shape that control the worst in us and bring out the best.

Z. Madison is certain if the unrestrained power of majority rule falls into the hands of a single-minded group, without any need for it to compromise with others, *"neither moral nor religious motives can be relied on as an adequate control"* of the majority's behavior (No. 10). This recognition that morality and religion need the help of wisely formed institutions is coupled with a faith that, if we *do* wisely design our politics, the good sense and sound morality of most people, grounded in their religious upbringing, will be the bedrock on which our constitutional order and our liberties rest:

*As there is a degree of depravity in mankind which
requires a certain degree of circumspection and distrust,
so there are other qualities in human nature, which justify
a certain portion of esteem and confidence. Republican
government presupposes the existence of these qualities in
a higher degree than any other form. Were the pictures
which have been drawn by the political jealousy of some
among us faithful likenesses of the human character, the
inference would be, that there is not sufficient virtue
among men for self-government; and that nothing less
than the chains of despotism can restrain them from
destroying and devouring one another.* (No. 55)

Madison is ultimately hopeful about human nature, or else he
could not endorse the idea of a democratic republic at all.

AA. The authors of the *Federalist Papers* assume, for all their
religious diversity, the American people are by and large the
children of a shared culture, with a shared moral foundation:

*Providence has been pleased to give this one connected
country to one united people — a people descended from
the same ancestors, speaking the same language,
professing the same religion, attached to the same
principles of government, very similar in their manners
and customs, and who, by their joint counsels, arms, and
efforts, fighting side by side throughout a long and bloody
war, have nobly established their general liberty and
independence.* (No. 2)

Certainly this statement exaggerates, for political purposes, the
degree of cultural, ancestral, and even linguistic sameness among
the Americans of 1787. Still, the essential teachings of the
Christian faith, the use of the English language as the common

speech nationwide, the inheritance of British legal principles and political traditions, and the shared and unifying experience of the Revolution made Americans into one people with a shared consciousness of a shared identity. As the nation matured after the Founding, it faced problems of assimilating new groups— immigrants from every land, emancipated slaves, and formerly independent Native Americans—into the American mix. Language, law, and a kind of "civic religion" melded elements of Judeo-Christian teaching with patriotic political principles, and became the essential tools of that assimilation. And, among these essential principles of the American psyche is the protection of full religious freedom for all, whatever their beliefs. As President George Washington said in a famous 1790 letter to the Jewish congregation of Newport, Rhode Island:

> *For happily, the Government of the United States, which gives to bigotry no sanction, to persecution no assistance requires only that they who live under its protection should demean themselves as good citizens, in giving it on all occasions their effectual support. . . . everyone shall sit in safety under his own vine and figtree and there shall be none to make him afraid.*

ABOUT THE AUTHORS & EDITORS

Scott D. Cosenza is an attorney and Policy Director at the educational and public policy organization One Generation Away. He is a graduate of the Villanova University School of Law, and co-author of *The Bill of Rights and You.*

J. Kennerly Davis, Jr. is Deputy Attorney General of Virginia, a graduate of the Harvard Law School, and an Adjunct Assistant Professor at the University of Richmond.

Christopher Donesa is Chief Counsel for the United States House of Representatives Permanent Select Committee on Intelligence. He is a graduate of the Duke Law School and Georgetown University.

Matthew J. Franck is Director of the Witherspoon Institute's William E. and Carol G. Simon Center on Religion and the Constitution. He is Professor Emeritus of Political Science at Radford University where he taught constitutional law, American politics, and political philosophy.

Claire M. Griffin spent 28 years as a high school history and government teacher before joining the Bill of Rights Institute, where she served as Vice President for Education. She is the principal of CGC, an independent consulting business working with non-profit organizations and government agencies to promote the goals of civic education.

Jamil N. Jaffer is Senior Counsel for the United States House of Representatives Permanent Select Committee on Intelligence and Adjunct Professor of Law at the George Mason University School of Law.

Evan M. Koster is an attorney who practices corporate and financial services law in New York. He is a graduate of the George Washington University School of Law and Brandeis University.

Robert T. Miller is Professor of Law and F. Arnold Daum Fellow in Corporate Law at the University of Iowa College of Law. Prior to his current position, he was Professor of Law at the Villanova University School of Law and the Associate Director and Acting Executive Director of the Matthew J. Ryan Center for the Study of Free Institutions and the Public Good at Villanova University.

Roger Pilon is the founder and director of the Cato Institute's Center for Constitutional Studies, where he holds the B. Kenneth Simon Chair in Constitutional Studies. In 1989 the Bicentennial Commission presented him with its Benjamin Franklin Award for excellence in writing on the U.S. Constitution. He is the publisher of the *Cato Supreme Court Review* and is an Adjunct Professor of government at Georgetown University.

Stephen B. Presser is the Raoul Berger Professor of Legal History at Northwestern University School of Law and Professor of Business Law at the Kellogg School of Management. He is co-author of *The American Constitutional Order: Introduction to the History and Nature of American Constitutional Law*.

John Shu is an attorney practicing in Southern California. He is a graduate of the Pepperdine University School of Law, and holds degrees from Peking University and the University of Pennsylvania. He has served in the White House under multiple Presidents.

William J. Watkins, Jr. is a Research Fellow at The Independent Institute and a legal scholar specializing in constitutional law and health law. He is the author of *Reclaiming the American Revolution: The Kentucky and Virginia Resolutions and Their Legacy*.

Federalist Papers Index

Federalist Number	Page Number(s)
52	81, 88
54	81
55	96
57	52, 57
63	36
68	39, 51
72	55, 57
78	42-44, 46-49, 82
79	45
81	46, 48, 49
84	53, 54, 70, 71, 92
85	84